MW01291156

RISE UP

AND

𝓑UILD

DEVOTIONAL

52 Inspirational Thoughts
for Dealing With Anxiety
and Depression

DANA RONGIONE

RISE UP
AND
*B*UILD
DEVOTIONAL

*52 Inspirational Thoughts for Dealing
With Anxiety and Depression*

DANA RONGIONE

All Scripture notations are taken from
The Holy Bible, KJV.

Copyright © 2017 Dana Rongione

All rights reserved. No part of this publication may be reproduced, distributed, or transmitted in any form or by any means, including photocopying, recording, or other electronic or mechanical methods, without the prior written permission of the publisher, except in the case of brief quotations embodied in reviews and certain other non-commercial uses permitted by copyright law.

How would you like to receive free devotions in your inbox every weekday?

No fees. No catch.
No obligations.

Sign up today at DanaRongione.com.

RISE UP AND BUILD

TABLE OF CONTENTS

A PERSONAL WORD FOR YOU

Before we even begin down this difficult road, I want you to know that I feel your pain. I know, all too well, what it's like to sit and cry for no reason at all. I've experienced panic attacks, stress headaches and pits of despair so deep that it seemed I would never again see the light of day.

In my book, **Rise Up and Build: A Biblical Approach to Dealing With Anxiety and Depression**, I share some of my deepest hurts and how the Lord inspired me to write about a topic I felt I'd been studying (and failing) for far too long. But with the inspiration, the good Lord gave me an education and enabled me to finally find the answers that had seemed elusive for so long. I no longer have to be a slave to my emotions or a prisoner to my ever-changing moods. I have a choice. . .and so do you.

The original **Rise Up and Build** book takes you by the hand and explores the necessary steps to overcome anxiety and depression in your life, but I didn't want to stop there. I don't know about you, but I get sick and tired of people giving me advice but never explaining to me how to implement that advice. Seriously? I want someone to take me by the hand and tell me what to do and how to do it. And that's why I've written this devotional.

Rise Up and Build is based on the book of Nehemiah and the rebuilding of the walls of Jerusalem. While the devotions in this book are taken from various passages in the Bible, the premise is taken from the book of Nehemiah.

And Ezra opened the book in the sight of all the people; (for he was above all the people;) and when he opened it, all the people stood up: And Ezra blessed the Lord, the great God. And all the people answered, Amen, Amen, with lifting up their hands: and they bowed their heads, and worshipped the Lord with their faces to the ground. . .So they read in the book in the law of God distinctly, and gave the sense, and caused them to understand the reading. (Nehemiah 8:5-6,8)

Building the wall was a good thing, but the people needed more. They needed motivation and inspiration, just like we do. And they found it in the Word of God. My purpose for writing this devotional is to inspire and encourage you as you work to build up the walls against anxiety and depression. I have chosen these specific devotions from some of the darkest times in my life to prove that, even in the darkness, God gives a song. There are fifty-two devotions in all, one for each day it took for the Israelites to rebuild the wall. Feel free to read one each day or several at a time. It's completely up to you. The idea is to keep your thoughts focused on God and what He's doing in and through you.

So, if you're ready to be changed from the inside out, I invite you to join me. Together, let us rise up and build!

Dana Rongione

THIS IS THE PITS!

And it came to pass, when Joseph was come unto his brethren, that they stript Joseph out of his coat, his coat of many colours that was on him; And they took him, and cast him into a pit: and the pit was empty, there was no water in it.
Genesis 37:23-24

      I had intended to share with my Sunday School class a lesson on the pit. As I sat down to study for the lesson, many thoughts had already begun to take shape. But the further into the study I went, the more the Lord changed my way of thinking. He brought to mind things that I never would have dreamed of, and I'm so glad He did. I was so blessed by the time I finished studying that I couldn't wait until Sunday when I could share it with my ladies. Today, I would like to share just a portion of it with you as well.

I'm sure you've heard the phrase, "Life is the pits" or "This is the pits." When we look up a few of the definitions of the word "pit," we can understand how those phrases came to be. Let's look at a few:

1) a hole, shaft, or cavity in the ground —In other words, a pit is a deep, dark place, surrounded by high walls and often filled with the stench of death, decay and stagnation. Well, that certainly describes how we feel from time to time, doesn't it? In a dark place. Surrounded by walls. Stagnant. Reeking of stinky attitudes. Hmm.

2) an area often sunken or depressed below the adjacent floor area—I don't know about how well the definition as a whole resonates with life, but I can definitely relate to the words "sunken" and "depressed." How about you?

3) a place or situation of futility, misery, or degradation—Wow, now we're really

getting somewhere. How many times have we found ourselves in futile situations? How often have we been downright miserable with our circumstances? How degrading is it to be stuck in a stinky, slimy pit and have no idea how to get out? Life is the pits? Yeah, sometimes it sure seems that way.

But this, my dear friend, is where it gets really good. If that were the last definition of the word "pit," this entire lesson would be more depressing than it would be encouraging. But, alas, there is another definition. One that, even though I knew of it, did not even cross my mind until I read it in the dictionary. And then, I had a bit of a shouting spell. Are you ready for it? Okay, here goes:

4) any of the areas alongside an auto racecourse used for refueling and repairing the cars during a race—Hallelujah!!! Doesn't the Bible say that we're in a race? (Hebrews 12:1-2) So often, we're inclined to think of the pit as a place of punishment or

torture, but the fact is that sometimes God places us in the pit (or allows us to be placed in the pit) because He knows we need to be refueled and repaired.

Now, I don't know much about auto racing. To be honest, the mere thought of it puts me to sleep. But I do know enough about it to understand that the drivers don't enjoy the time in the pit. Why? Because they'd rather be racing. However, they know the pit is a necessary part of the race. Refueling and repairing have to be done in order for the drivers to finish the course.

We are no different. We have a race to run, and we can't do that when we're falling apart and running on fumes. So God, in His great mercy, provides time in the pit. Time to refuel, refresh, and repair. Time to regain perspective. Time to refocus. It's not a punishment; it's a privilege.

Perhaps you're in a pit right now, glancing up at the high walls surrounding you and wondering if you'll ever again see the light of day. Maybe you're questioning what you've done wrong and why you're being punished. Perhaps you're even angry at God for leaving you in such a desolate place. If so, take heart. You're actually in a good position. God is preparing you to finish the work He's called you to do. He has great plans for you, and this pit stop is just one way He's enabling you to finish the race.

Oh, and one more thing about the pit. Keep in mind that it is not a destination but rather a rest stop along the way. Joseph was raised from the pit. So was David. You will be too.

He brought me up also out of an horrible pit, out of the miry clay, and set my feet upon a rock, and established my goings.
Psalm 40:2

RISE UP AND BUILD

LIVING OUT MY OWN FICTIONAL TALE

May I confide in you? Some days—more often than I would care to admit—I feel like my own personal version of Dr. Jekyll and Mr. Hyde. You remember the literary tale, right? Dr. Jekyll was a brilliant scientist who was so distraught by the evil within himself that he created a potion, intending to strip the evil from his body, leaving him good and clean and right. Only, as is the case with most "magic potions," it didn't work. Instead of cleaving the wickedness from himself, he essentially cleaved his personality in two, leaving one good, wholesome man and one evil monster of a man. Each character fought for control of the single body, and the life of Dr. Jekyll became a life-long battle to remain dominate over Mr. Hyde.

Like Jekyll, I am often distraught over the horrible things buried deep within my heart. Every now and then, my mask of godliness will slip, and I'll catch a glimpse of things so dark and horrible that I have to turn away. I see billows of bitterness and resentment. I hear whispers of pride and arrogance. A lack of compassion. Love missing in action. And the thoughts, oh the thoughts that run rampant through my brain. It's enough to send me seeking my own magic potion to rid myself of such unholiness.

I guess the truth is that we are all a bit like Dr. Jekyll and Mr. Hyde. When Jesus saved us, he severed sin's hold over us and gave us power over it, which means that we no longer have to sin. It is in our nature, but we are no longer slaves to it. However, because it is in our nature, and we still live in bodies of flesh, that sin nature still lies just under the surface, waiting for an opportunity to assert itself and take control. Mr. Hyde (or in our case, Mr. Flesh) represents all the worst parts of ourselves that we would rather just go away. But until the return of Christ, when we can shed these earthly vessels, there's no escaping the presence of Mr. Flesh, but that's not to say that we can't escape his power. And the key to that escape lies in Christ.

As I said, when we asked Jesus to save us, He severed sin's hold on us, but to be daily delivered from the power of sin, we have to make a choice—serve God or serve flesh. The truth is, we can't do both because our flesh doesn't want the same thing that God wants. Every day, hour after hour, we have to determine that we will not give in to our fleshly desires, thoughts or attitudes but instead, we will honor God in everything that we do. Just like Jekyll, we're in for a life-long battle, but unlike the mad scientist, we don't have to face it alone. God is our strength. He is our help. He will give us what we need to defend ourselves against—well, ourselves. He will provide us with the power to say "yes" to the good and "no" to the bad. It is He alone that can give us victory over Mr. Flesh.

What about you? Do you feel like Dr. Jekyll and Mr. Hyde? Do you find yourself examining your spiritual walk and cringing because you feel you should be further along? Do you sometimes frustrate yourself by the ungodly things you do? If so, you're in good company, but take heart because there is hope. While we cannot rid ourselves of this fleshly nature, we can control it by the power of God. And He is offering us the power if we'll only accept it. Don't try to face Mr. Flesh alone. He's a formidable foe, and if we're not careful, he will take over. Fortunately, though the flesh is strong, God is stronger. Tell Him your troubles. Seek His help. And allow Him to help you fight off Mr. Flesh. You'll be glad you did!

This I say then, Walk in the Spirit, and ye shall not fulfil the lust of the flesh. For the flesh lusteth against the Spirit, and the Spirit against the flesh: and these are contrary the one to the other: so that ye cannot do the things that ye would.
Galatians 5:16-17

RISE UP AND BUILD

DO YOU SEE A WEED OR A WISH?

Whether we enjoy life or simply endure it boils down to one thing: perspective. How we view our circumstances—both good and bad—determines how we act and react in our daily walk. We have a tendency to focus on the bad. We put a magnifying glass on how things are "supposed to be" according to our own warped view of how our lives should play out. But, how many times do we stop to examine the things that did work out in our lives when, according to all the evidence, they shouldn't have worked out at all?

For example, I have, on multiple occasions, tried to create a financial budget for our family. According to all the money experts, creating a budget helps us to stay within the bounds of our financial state and even save money in the long run. There's only one problem: every time I budget, the numbers end up in the red. EVERY TIME!!!! Yep, when I enter in how much we make and how much we spend on essentials like tithe, groceries, gas, utilities, mortgage, etc., the math simply doesn't work. Yet, "somehow" the bills get paid. According to the budget, it shouldn't work; nevertheless, it does. . . time and time again.

What about that one in a million opportunity that seemed to fall in your lap? By all odds, that shouldn't have happened, but it did. What about the cancer that disappeared when the doctors had given up all hope? What about the people who have walked again when the specialists stated that they were paralyzed for life? What about the miracles we see every day? Why isn't our magnifying glass focused on them instead of our troubles? One word—perspective!

It's a lot like looking at a dandelion. No doubt, in a just a few more weeks, we'll have about a million of them in our yard. So when I look out across the property, what will I see—a million weeds or a million wishes? You've wished upon a dandelion, right? It's a lot like making a birthday wish instead of blowing out candles, you blow all the little white fluffy things (my scientific term) off the dandelion in a single breath. If you place a child and an adult in a field of dandelions, you'll undoubtedly see two opposing reactions. The adult will turn up his nose and possibly even sniffle a little if he has allergies. The child, on the other hand, will pick a "flower" and blow. Then do it again and again and again, each time accompanied by a chorus of giggles. Who is enjoying the experience and who is enduring it?

The Bible says we are to have childlike faith, and I believe that, when it comes to our perspectives, we will do well to be more child-like. See the good, not the bad. Examine all the times things worked out better than anticipated instead of the times they worked out worse. Magnify the pleasant things in life, not the troubles. Focus on the wishes, not the weeds.

Open thou mine eyes, that I may behold
wondrous things out of thy law.
Psalm 119:18

ARE YOU DELIGHTING IN BLESSING?

As he loved cursing, so let it come unto him:
as he delighted not in blessing,
so let it be far from him.
Psalm 109:17

In the above psalm, David is speaking of the wicked, but I have to admit that the latter half of that verse gave me pause: *as he delighted not in blessing, so let it be far from him*. In essence, David was saying, "Since he doesn't acknowledge his blessings anyway, stop sending them." And that smote my heart to the very core.

How often do we take our blessings for granted? How many times do the blessings come, and we merely nod our heads

27

like that was exactly what was supposed to happen? Why is it that it is so much easier to remember our troubles than it is our blessings? Could it be that we, like the wicked David spoke of, are failing to delight in our blessings?

Sure, we may send up a quick prayer of thanks. And yes, we'll often tell a few people about what God did for us. But then another day passes and instead of being thankful for what we have already received, we start looking to God and asking for more. Shameful, isn't it? What's worse is that Satan can get us so bamboozled that we begin to doubt that we have any blessings at all. It goes something like this:

"Yes, I have a roof over my head, but unfortunately, it leaks."

"It's true the Lord allowed us to replace the washing machine, but now the dryer is acting up."

"Yes, the Lord has always met our needs, but things are tighter than ever, and I don't see any way out."

Do you see how easy it is to bypass the blessing in order to find a reason to complain? I don't know why we do it, but it seems to be our natural tendency. I don't know about you, but I am desperately feeling the need for a change of tactics. I believe it's time to kick some "buts" out of my life and focus only on the blessings.

"Yes, I have a roof over my head." Stop!

"It's true the Lord allowed us to replace the washing machine." Stop!

"Yes, the Lord has always met our needs." Stop!

It sounds a bit like I'm trying to send a telegram, but I think you get my point. Don't state a blessing then negate it by saying, "but. . ." State the blessing and focus on that blessing lest God take David's advice and stop sending the blessings altogether.

RISE UP AND BUILD

THE WORRIER'S 23RD PSALM

A few days ago, my Song of the Day choice was "The Warrior Is a Child." There is a reason I chose that particular song. You see, on Monday, I had a bit of an emotional breakdown. I was extremely tired from a busy weekend, and as I faced the prospect of another hectic week, I lost it. As I cried on Jason's shoulder, I tried to explain my feelings and frustrations but, to be honest, I didn't think I was making much sense. Evidently, though, I was because he pulled out his phone, pressed a few buttons, then placed the phone in my hand. He had pulled up a video of "The Warrior Is a Child." As I listened/watched, I cried that much more. The song conveyed the exact message I was trying to get across. So many people look to me for answers and encouragement, and that's fine. But some days, this warrior gets weary and needs some encouragement as well.

While I watched the video, Jason went out to the kitchen to fix me some breakfast. (Is he a gem or what?) When the video was through, I met him in the kitchen and tried to smile. "That's pretty accurate," I said, "although right now I feel like the line should be *the **worrier** is a child*." He laughed, and I did too, but deep down I was cringing because I knew it was too true.

This morning, as the Lord dealt with my heart about my tendency to worry, I wondered what Psalm 23 would sound like if David had written it during one of his downward spirals into despair rather than on one of his "up days." (Yes, I know. I wonder about strange things.) Anyway, this is what I came up with. I call it *The Worrier's 23rd Psalm*.

Anxiety is my shepherd,
and I never have all I need.
It maketh me to lie down
in sleepless frustration.
It leadeth me beside the
tumultuous waves.
It exhausts my soul.
It leadeth me in the paths of despair
for its name's sake.
Yea, though I walk through the
valley of the shadow of death,
I will fear all the more.
For anxiety is ever with me.
The chocolate and caffeine,
they comfort me.
Anxiety preparest a table before me
in the presence of mine enemies.
It anointest my head
with devastating thoughts.
My frustration runneth over.
Surely, despair and sickness shall follow me all
the days of my life,
And I shall dwell in the
pit of hopelessness forever.

I'm sure we wouldn't hear that passage quoted in many church services, now would we? Unfortunately, it's all too familiar to some of us. No, we may not put it in those words—or any words, for that matter. But we display it by our actions and attitudes.

By adjusting this psalm to the worrier's viewpoint, I ruined it. I turned something beautiful into something hideous. Something comforting into something depressing. I made it exactly the opposite of what God intended for it to be. When we worry, we do the same thing. We turn our lives into the opposite of what God has in mind for us. He longs for us to focus on Him, but we're too busy looking at our problems. We destroy the loveliness and comfort that we could have if only we would trust the Lord.

I was reminded twice recently that if you hold a coin up in front of your face in the right way, that coin can actually block out the entire sun. Our worries do the same thing. They block out the SON. Let's be careful. Worry is a drain on our time, energy, and health. It is also a sin. Trust God today. He's earned it!

The Lord is my strength and my shield; my heart trusted in him, and I am helped: therefore my heart greatly rejoiceth; and with my song will I praise him.
Psalm 28:7

RISE UP AND BUILD

WATCH OUT FOR THE SNAKE!

Earlier last week, while on my morning prayer walk, I came upon a baby snake. Yes, the scaly intruder was on the walking path not in the woods where he belonged. Yes, he gave me quite a scare. And yes, I did my best to avoid him. I don't do snakes!!!!

On Friday, as I again went about my merry way, pouring my heart out to God and enjoying the lovely weather, I was met by three approaching bicyclists, who each warned me about a snake on the trail ahead. I thanked them and acted as if it were no big deal, but immediately, I was on full alert. My mind spun. Was it the same baby snake I'd seen earlier in the week? Could they have seen such a small snake from their bikes at that speed?   Was the snake on the trail or just off to the side? What kind of snake are we talking about? And how big?

No matter how hard I tried, I could no longer focus on my prayers. My eyes darted back and forth across the trail. I searched the grass on either side. I watched for any movement. That silly snake became all I could think about, and here's the real kicker —I never found it! Nope, all the way back, I searched and expected the snake, but I never came across it. Either the bicyclists had scared it enough that it returned to its natural habitat, or it was only crossing the road to get to the other side (no chicken jokes here, I promise). Whatever the case, he was nowhere to be found, and I lost a good twenty minutes of my prayer time over that creepy critter.

Fortunately, the Lord also used the situation to teach me a valuable lesson. There is a reason He doesn't tell us about every bend in the road ahead and every heartache that is awaiting us. There is a purpose for him not showing us the master blueprint of our lives, complete with all its twists and turns, ups and downs. And the reason is this: that's all we would concentrate on.

If we knew there was a pitfall ahead, we would spend all of our time thinking about it. What kind of pitfall will it be? Is it big or small? Is it similar to something I've been through before? We would watch and wait, at every turn expecting to come upon trouble. And just as my snake-watching did, that intense focus would rob us of our joy, energy and time with God. It would overwhelm us. Anxiety and anticipation would permeate every fiber of our being to where we would be just about useless in accomplishing anything else.

Once I was off the trail Friday, and back in my neighborhood, I spent the rest of the walk home praising God for this beautiful reminder. I don't need to see the future; I only need to trust the One who holds it. And despite how many times I think I want to know all the answers, Friday's snake encounter (or snake non-encounter, as the case turned out to be) reminds me that knowing is not always that great a thing. After all, if I hadn't known there was a snake ahead, I would have continued in my prayer time and enjoyed my beautiful morning walk. Knowing about that crazy snake changed everything: my focus, my attitude and my gaze.

My friend, sometimes it's hard to face the unknown. I get that. I do. But now I see that sometimes it's better not to know. It's better to trust the One who does. He understands the dangers ahead, and He'll keep us from harm.   And when life seems overwhelming, remember that not only does Jesus know the way, He is the way! That's all we need to know.

*Commit thy way unto the Lord; trust also in
him; and he shall bring it to pass.
Psalm 37:5*

RISE UP AND BUILD

ARE YOU SINGING OR SULKING?

In Exodus 15, the first twenty-one verses outline a song of praise and victory from Moses and the children of Israel. God had just delivered them through the Red Sea and from the hand of the Egyptian army, and needless to say, the people had reason to rejoice. So, for twenty-one verses they lift up their voice in praise, thanking God for who He is and what He is capable of doing. The song is specific, thorough and heartfelt, and though I don't have the time or space to type out the entire song here, I would like to share with you verse two: *The Lord is my strength and song, and he is become my salvation: he is my God, and I will prepare him an habitation; my father's God, and I will exalt him.* Keep this verse in mind because we will come back to it in a minute.

Now, I want you to take a look at what happens in the next few verses. *So Moses brought Israel from the Red sea, and they went out into the wilderness of Shur; and they went three days in the wilderness, and found no water. And when they came to Marah, they could not drink of the waters of Marah, for they were bitter: therefore the name of it was called Marah. And the people murmured against Moses, saying, What shall we drink? (vs. 22-24)*

Three days! Within three days, the miracle of the Red Sea had been forgotten. The praises of God had been replaced with murmurs and complaints. In fact, it's safe to say that the water wasn't the only thing that was bitter that day. There were a lot of bitter attitudes as well. What happened? What could have possibly changed so much in three days that their singing turned into sulking?

For starters, their circumstances changed. No longer were they standing on the edge of victory, but they were wandering around in a desert of defeat and despair. Secondly, their attitudes changed. Where earlier they had been full of joy and relief at their deliverance from Egypt, now all they could focus on was their hunger, thirst and fatigue. But do you realize what didn't change? God did not change. The God who delivered them safely across the Red Sea was the same God who was leading them in the wilderness. The God to whom they sang praise and honor and worship was still just as deserving of their song. Though their circumstances and attitudes had changed, God was still God, and as they stated in their own song, He was still their strength, their song and their salvation. How quickly they had forgotten.

But I'm afraid we have no right to judge, for we often do the same thing. When things are going well and we're walking in victory, it's easy to praise God and thank Him for who He is and all He's done. But after a few days in the wilderness, when our circumstances have changed, our attitudes grow bitter just like the waters of Marah. We forget all about our victory. We lose track of our song. And it seems all we can focus on is what's wrong in our lives instead of remembering all the things that God has brought us through in the past. We concentrate on the things in our lives that are ever-changing instead of focusing on the One who never changes. And then, like the children of Israel, we begin to murmur.

Are you wandering in the wilderness today? Does victory seem far from your grasp? Are defeat and despair bearing down on you? If so, I remind you that this too shall pass. Your circumstances and negative feelings are not here to stay. They will shift and change as an autumn leaf on a windy day, so don't put too much stock in them. Instead, I urge you to focus on the One who never changes. He was faithful yesterday, and He will be faithful again today. He has seen you through the tough times, and He's not about to forsake you now. Hang in there, and whatever you do, don't lose your song!

RISE UP AND BUILD

SOMETIMES WEAKER IS BETTER

Sixteen years old was Uzziah when he began to reign, and he reigned fifty and two years in Jerusalem. His mother's name also was Jecoliah of Jerusalem. And he did that which was right in the sight of the Lord, according to all that his father Amaziah did.
II Chronicles 26:3-4

If you've read through the list of Israel's and Judah's kings in the books of Kings and Chronicles, then you'll know that the phrase "did that which was right in the sight of the Lord" is, unfortunately, an uncommon phrase. Yes, it's in there a few times, but more often than not, the Bible tells us that the kings did that which was evil in the sight of the Lord. Honestly, it gets depressing. But now and then, there arose a king that trusted the Lord and did His will, and Uzziah was one of those kings. . . for a while.

Second Chronicles 26 details how Uzziah sought God, and because of that reliance, God made him prosper (v. 5). The chapter also tells us that God helped Uzziah in the fights against his enemies (v. 7). The Scripture talks about how much Uzziah accomplished during his reign because of God's aid and blessing. Unfortunately, in verse 16, the story takes a horrific turn: *But when he was strong, his heart was lifted up to his destruction: for he transgressed against the Lord his God, and went into the temple of the Lord to burn incense upon the altar of incense.*

Everyone knew that only the priests could go into the temple and burn incense. It was their job. It was God's command. It had been that way since the temple and priesthood began. But Uzziah didn't care about God's rules anymore. Evidently, all his prosperity had gone to his head, and Uzziah had started to think that he was "somebody." Like Nebuchadnezzar, he looked around at his kingdom and accomplishments and said, "Wow! Look at what I've done! I must be the best king ever!" God knocked Nebuchadnezzar off his self-appointed pedestal by turning him into some form of a beast that lived off the land. He humbled Uzziah by striking him with leprosy—a disease that remained until Uzziah's death.

There is a reason the Bible warns us over and over again about pride. God hates it, and it's dangerous—not just to us, but to others as well. Not only that, but I want to take particular notice of the phrasing the Bible used, *But when he was strong, his heart was lifted up to his destruction*. When he was strong. When I read that phrase, I thought of Paul's thorn. Though the Bible doesn't specify the nature of Paul's thorn, it tells us why the thorn was there. In fact, it tells us twice in the same verse: *And lest I should be exalted above measure through the abundance of the revelations, there was given to me a thorn in the flesh, the messenger of Satan to buffet me, lest I should be exalted above measure. (II Corinthians 12:7)*

The purpose of Paul's thorn was to keep him weak and humble, and I dare say that the purpose of our thorns may be the same. You see, when we're weak, we're dependent on God. We stay close to Him. We lean on Him for strength. Our thorns serve as reminders that we cannot make it on our own. Without them, we're in danger of becoming like Uzziah or Nebuchadnezzar. In that perfect world where everything goes our way, who needs God, right?

I don't know about your thorn, but I know about my own. I know how many times I've begged and cried to the Lord to remove it. I understand how often I've felt hindered from doing the things I want to do for the Lord because of my thorn. I feel the heartache each morning when I awake to realize the thorn is still present. But after reading today's passage in II Chronicles, I see things differently. If it takes a thorn to keep me humble and dependent on God, then I'll bear the thorn gladly because the alternative is unacceptable. Yes, I see now sometimes weaker is better!

RISE UP AND BUILD

.

ARE THERE "MENTS" ON YOUR PILLOW?

Have you ever been to a fancy hotel? You know, the kind where they leave mints on your pillow. I don't think I have, but that's okay. I'm not a fancy hotel kind of girl. Frankly, I'd rather stay in a cabin in the woods, but maybe that's just me. Besides, it's probably a good thing that I don't crave that kind of hotel stay because I'm pretty sure I couldn't afford it.

I did, however, go to bed with "ments" on my pillow last night, but let me tell you, they were not the kind of mints one desires, and they did not leave a pleasant taste in my mouth. No, I'm afraid the "ments" on my pillow were discouragement, discontentment and disagreement. You know how it is, you fall into bed at the end of a long day. You're exhausted. You crave sleep like Cookie Monster craves chocolate chips. But the minute your head hits the pillow, you're assaulted with a million thoughts, most of them negative.

For me, it was discontentment over the leaky roof that had consumed much of our time, energy and patience over the weekend. It was discouragement over the aches and pains of my body that haven't given me a moment's peace for months. It was disagreement with God over the definition of "good" because at that point in time, I didn't see any of these things working out for my good like He promised they would in Romans 8:28.

Guess what! After sucking on those "ments" all that time before finally drifting off to sleep, I awoke this morning to an exhausted body and a weary spirit. It turns out that these "ments" don't dissolve when you suck on them; they grow. The more time we spend with them, the bigger they become.

The more we think about them and dwell on them, the more of our time and energy they eat up. And let me tell you, unlike other mints, these turn sour rather quickly.

So, how do we avoid the "ments" on our pillows? How do we overcome the discouragement, discontentment and disagreements in our lives? Well, first off, we can't ignore them and hope they'll go away. Trust me, that doesn't work. We must deal with them but through the strength and grace of God. We must take them to God, just as we would any other burden, and explain that they are too heavy for us to bear. Then, with all sincerity and commitment, we must give them over to Him and walk away. Yep, I'm quoting Elsa from *Frozen* again, "Let it go, let it go!"

Seriously, we will all face discouragement, discontentment and disagreements from time to time. Often, we may face them all at once, and the result can be overwhelming. But the fact is that we don't have to suck on those "ments." Acknowledge them, and then let them go. Hand them over the One who can actually do something about them. And then, maybe we can get the peaceful sleep we so deeply desire.

As soon as you have the chance, make yourself a note and leave it on your pillow. When you go to bed tonight, you'll have a written reminder to cast your burdens on the Lord before crawling under the covers and attempting to sleep. What should the note say? That's up to you, but I'll tell you what mine says: "Hold the *ments*, please!"

I laid me down and slept; I awaked;
for the Lord sustained me.
Psalm 3:5

RETRAIN THE BRAIN

Have I mentioned how much I dislike trailblazing? Hiking? Love it! Trailblazing? Not so much. But I've recently discovered that I need to step outside of my comfort zone and do some major trailblazing through my mind. You're probably wondering what in the world I'm talking about, right? Let me see if I can explain.

Think of your brain as a forest. There are many trees, flowers, plants and other resources. We know them as thoughts, feelings, signals, etc. To reach (or access) any of these resources, we must go down the trail that leads to the desired resource. As with forest trails, some of our minds' trails are used frequently and are well-marked and easy to follow. Others, however, are not traveled as frequently and become a little harder to spot and maneuver. Does that make sense?

In my mind, the trails leading to fear, worry, discouragement, anger, bitterness, frustration and negative thoughts are well-marked and unfortunately, well-trodden. In fact, they are so obvious that I often find myself traveling down them without even realizing how I got there. There are other trails that are covered with debris and cobwebs—trails for which I must search if I am to travel them. These trails include those leading to happiness, contentment, positive thinking, self-discipline and a host of other good traits. Somehow, over the years, I've allowed those trails to become overgrown. And because of their state of disarray, I've found it easier and more convenient to walk on the paths that are well-blazed. After all, why make more work for myself, right?

Over the past couple of months, the Lord has been dealing with me about several things in my life that are not as they should be. Nothing major, mind you, but things that bring me shame, nonetheless. For example, the healthy living I started last year only lasted until a major crisis hit. Then, I ran back to my comfort food, and I've been holding on to it ever since. That kind of thing. Stuff that won't mean a thing to you, but it certainly means a lot to me.

And do you want to know why these things are out of sorts? Because my thinking is out of sorts. By frequenting the familiar pathways in my brain, I'm allowing all the wrong things to dictate my thoughts, feeling and actions. The comfortable place says, "I just can't do this." The hidden paths say, "I can do ALL things through Christ because He gives me strength." Time and time again, I'm heeding all the wrong advice when I know the right advice is in there somewhere. So, it's time to retrain the brain. It's time to blaze some new trails and to take back some of the ones that have been overgrown. It's time to quit being so concerned with being comfortable and instead concern myself with following the Lord's will. Out with the old and in with the new!

And the best place to start is with God's Word. The more I fill my brain with His promises, the less room there will be for Satan's lies. With God's Word in my heart, I'll have a much easier time controlling my thoughts and actions.

And be not conformed to this world: but be
ye transformed by the renewing of your
mind, that ye may prove what is that good,
and acceptable, and perfect, will of God.
Romans 12:2

WHY IS GOD PUTTING ME THROUGH THE FIRE?

Have you ever used coconut oil? It's amazing stuff and extremely healthy. One thing I find so fascinating about it is that it's solid most of the time. Only above certain temperatures (somewhere around 76 degrees) does it become liquid. So, in its solid state, it's like butter. You can spread it on toast or a baked potato. You can scoop out spoonfuls to top your casserole. Or, if you're into using healthy cosmetics, you can use the oil as soap, moisturizer or deodorant. Awesome stuff!

Unfortunately, I haven't been able to deal with coconut oil in its solid state since the temperatures here in upstate South Carolina began to rise a few weeks ago. Our old air conditioner is not wanting to play nice this year, and until we can get it fixed (or find an alternate solution), the inside temperature isn't much cooler than the outside, which means my coconut oil has remained in a liquid state. But, you know what? That's okay because I've discovered many instances where the liquid form works just fine and some occasions where it works even better than it did as a solid. For example, as a moisturizer, I've found that the liquid allows me to get just the right amount without leaving my skin too oily. I also discovered that I didn't have to melt the oil first before preparing my little tablets for oil pulling (it's a health thing). Plus the liquid oil makes an excellent addition to the formula I use to make my all-natural makeup remover wipes. Yes, I'm finding that the liquid oil has many uses, some of which I would never have thought of when it was in its solid state.

A few weeks ago, though, when I first noticed my soupy oil, I thought, *Great! I can't use my favorite oil. The heat has ruined it and made it unusable.* But what I discovered was that the oil wasn't unusable at all but rather usable in different ways. As I mentioned earlier, I could use the oil for various purposes and even situations in which I had used it before and found that the liquid works better. Who knew?

God did. This concept is not new to Him. He is familiar with the process of turning up the heat in our lives. Not to ruin us. Not to destroy us. Not to make us unusable. But rather to equip us to be used for a different purpose or even to be used better for the same purposes. Just as silver is tried in the fire to rid it of its impurities, so are we tried to make us the best that we can be. It isn't a punishment or some cruel cosmic joke. Once again, God is doing all things for our good, and part of that good is being able to be used in ways that we (and others) never imagined.

Perhaps you're walking through the fire today, wondering if God really cares for you at all. My friend, He cares. Otherwise, He wouldn't take the time to make and mold you into what you ought to be. Don't fight the heat. Embrace it, knowing that God is preparing you to be used in ways that exceed your imagination. He has big plans for you if you'll only allow Him to finish His work in you.

For thou, O God, hast proved us: thou hast tried us, as silver is tried. Thou broughtest us into the net; thou laidst affliction upon our loins. Thou hast caused men to ride over our heads; we went through fire and through water: but thou broughtest us out into a wealthy place.
Psalm 66:10-12

ARE YOU GIVING GOD YOUR BEST?

Ye said also, Behold, what a weariness is it! and ye have snuffed at it, saith the Lord of hosts; and ye brought that which was torn, and the lame, and the sick; thus ye brought an offering: should I accept this of your hand? saith the Lord.
Malachi 1:13

I, for one, am glad that I don't have to sacrifice an animal every time I sin. For one thing, as an animal lover, I would be mortified to have to take the life of some precious creature. I am also not a fan of blood and gore, so I'm not sure how well I would hold up under such circumstances. That being said, however, I would like to think that if it were necessary, I would rise to the occasion and do as God commanded. At the point of time in which our passage was written, the children of Israel were not doing that.

In short, they had grown weary of the practice. They were tired of the offerings. They were sick of trying to find the perfect gift to give a holy God, so they began to take shortcuts. They continued the offerings, but with a half-hearted effort. They put little time and thought into what they were bringing and had a "good enough" attitude toward the entire process. The problem is, it wasn't good enough. God demanded a perfect sacrifice not some unenthusiastic effort.

Even though we are no longer required to offer animal sacrifices, the Bible says that we are to present ourselves as living sacrifices unto God (Romans 12:1). Once again, God demands our best, but is that what we are offering? Are we giving of ourselves fully unto God each and every day? Are we surrendering our lives, thoughts, attitudes and actions to His will, or are we fulfilling our own agenda, giving Him just enough control to ease our conscience? Are we giving of our tithe and our talents? How much are we offering to God as a living sacrifice?

In our passage above, the Lord asked the children of Israel, "Should I accept this of your hand?" I believe the Lord is asking each of us the same question. We attend church every Sunday and say it's good enough. We read our Bible a couple of times a week and think we're doing well. We say a prayer here and there and feel as if we're doing God a favor by talking to Him. We occasionally help out a friend in need and see ourselves as super-spiritual. But all along, we know we can do more—that we should do more—and God knows too.

The crazy thing is, we expect God to simply accept what were willing to give and be happy about it, but He's not. The truth is, He's disappointed. Yes, He still loves us, and that love will remain forever unchanged, but God's feelings towards us when we don't do our best are the same as they were toward the church of Laodicea. *I know thy works, that thou art neither cold nor hot: I would thou wert cold or hot. So then because thou art lukewarm, and neither cold nor hot, I will spue thee out of my mouth. (Revelation 3:15-16)*

I know it sounds harsh, but if we look at this passage literally, God says that our half-hearted efforts make Him sick. Is that what we want? Do we want to sicken or disappoint our holy God who was willing to give His only Son for us and asks for so little in return?

I know we live busy lives, and with so many things to do, it's tempting to cut corners here and there, but I caution you to remember that God is expecting your very best. He loves you, and not only does He want what's best <u>for</u> you, but He also wants what's best <u>from</u> you. Is He not worthy? Is He not deserving of all that we have to give? Please keep that in mind the next time you're tempted to do less than your best or to give less than what is required. God will bless your efforts, but only when you do your best! After all, it is our reasonable service!

RISE UP AND BUILD

GOD ALWAYS COMES THROUGH

I have to share with you what happened earlier this week. As usual, my mom was preparing for the annual ladies' meeting at the church she attends, and as I typically do, I agreed to help her set up. Shortly after I arrived to help on Monday afternoon, I discovered that things were falling apart. Some of the supplies were missing. Due to a miscommunication, the baked cookies that were supposed to go in the gift bags would not be there until the following day—the day of the meeting. And worst of all, the speaker for the meeting had called to say that she wasn't sure if she could make it to the meeting due to an emergency with her husband's health.

Rightfully so, my mom was flustered. Exhausted from her recent travels to help with my grandmother, she didn't even have the energy to cry, but I could tell she wanted to. I wanted to cry for her. As she always does, she had put a lot of time and energy into getting ready for this event and now, because of situations beyond anyone's control, everything was falling apart.

As I sat there staring at the fatigue and frustration in her eyes, I felt the prompting of the Lord. "I don't mind speaking at the meeting if you need someone to fill in." I couldn't believe the words that came out of my mouth! Did I just volunteer to speak at a ladies' meeting with one day's notice?

"You wouldn't have time to get anything ready," my sweet mother replied.

"It may not fit your theme, but I'm sure I could pull out one of my Sunday School lessons and make it work." What in the world? I felt like the dummy in a ventriloquist act. My mouth was moving, but I was certain those words weren't coming from me. . . or were they? Despite being amazed at my apparent eagerness to be put on the spot (which I usually despise), I felt calm and at ease. "Really, I don't mind."

Relief showed on her face. "Well, the theme for this year is love."

All I could do was laugh. Would you believe that my Sunday School lessons for the past three weeks have been about love? "Are you serious?" I smiled. "I think I can handle that."

We praised the Lord for His goodness and provision, went about the rest of our preparations and made plans for the following day. I was prepared to show up for the meeting ready to speak just in case the scheduled speaker couldn't make it. . . which, as it turns out, she couldn't.

All during the meeting Tuesday, I sat amazed at how well everything fit together. The songs fit right in with my lesson, even though they had never been intended to go together. Testimonies complimented the songs. The specials went right along with the testimonies. It was as if a puzzle was being completed right before our eyes, and the crazy thing was that the pieces had all come from different places.

Isn't that just like God? He met a need before we even realized there was one. He worked it out so that I would be at this point of study in my Sunday School class so that the topic would be fresh on my mind. He inspired the songs to be sung and the testimonies to be declared. And He wove it all together into a beautiful master-piece that I believe brought Him honor and glory. Even when everything seemed to be falling apart, God sent a wonderful reminder that He has everything under control. Once again, God reminded me that all things work together for good to those who love Him. He's taking care of us even when we may not see it because that's just the way He is.

How about we take time today to praise Him!

The Lord thy God in the midst of thee is mighty; he will save, he will rejoice over thee with joy; he will rest in his love, he will joy over thee with singing.
Zephaniah 3:17

RISE UP AND BUILD

IS YOUR BATTLE PLAN IN PLACE?

In II Chronicles 20, a group of warring nations bonded together in an assault on the nation of Judah. When Jehoshaphat, the current king, heard of the mob that was coming, he fell to his knees and sought the Lord. (Let me stop right here and say that the best battle plans begin with prayer.) Anyway, the king prayed, and the King of Kings answered with a four-step plan to win the victory over the invading armies.

Ye shall not need to fight in this battle: set yourselves, stand ye still, and see the salvation of the Lord with you, O Judah and Jerusalem: fear not, nor be dismayed; to morrow go out against them: for the Lord will be with you. And Jehoshaphat bowed his head with his face to the ground: and all Judah and the inhabitants of Jerusalem fell before the Lord, worshipping the Lord. (II Chronicles 20:17-18)

Step one: Wait!

Ye shall not need to fight in this battle: set yourselves, stand ye still.—When the enemy is coming for us, the last thing we want to do is wait. Run? Sure. Fight? Maybe. Plan? Definitely. But wait? Wait for the enemy to catch up with us? It makes no sense to us, and it goes against every fiber of our being. We want to do something—anything! Surely, the army of Judah was thinking about donning armor, sharpening weapons and securing the city as much as possible. But God said, "No, you're not fighting this one. This battle is mine. You just sit tight for now." How many times has God said the same to us?

Step two: Watch!

. . . see the salvation of the Lord with you, O Judah and Jerusalem.—There are

times when God wants us to get involved with the work and times when He wants us to sit back and watch what He can do. He doesn't need our participation. He doesn't require our best-laid plans. The battle is His, and He intends to fight it His way. But He wants to make sure we're paying attention because He knows we'll need the memories of this victory when we face the next battle.

Step three: Worry not!

. . .fear not, nor be dismayed; to mor-row go out against them: for the Lord will be with you.—God told Judah, "I've got this. Don't you worry about it." I don't know about you, but I've heard God whisper those same words to me on many occasions. When the days are dark, the bills are overdue, or the diagnosis is bad, worry seems like an appro-priate response. But it's not. In fact, it's not even really a response; it's a reaction. A re-sponse is how we act after thinking through a situation and considering all the factors. A

reaction is how we act before taking the time to think through a situation. It happens before we even realize it. We don't mean to worry; it just seems to happen. But God warns us about it so we'll be better prepared to recognize it and stop it in its tracks.

Step four: Worship!

And Jehoshaphat bowed his head with his face to the ground: and all Judah and the inhabitants of Jerusalem fell before the Lord, worshiping the Lord.—It's easy for us to praise and worship God after the battle has been won, but in the passage in II Chronicles, Judah and its king worshiped God before the battle even began. God said, "Don't worry. I'll take care of this one. You just sit back and watch." And Judah's response was heartfelt praise—not because of what God had done, but rather because of what He said He would do. Hasn't God said He would supply our every need? Hasn't He promised to take care of us just as He

82

promised He would take care of Judah? Hasn't He vowed to fight our battles? Yes, yes and yes. So why aren't we down on our knees in heartfelt praise?

Life is full of battles. Some are physical while others are spiritual. Some are emotional while others are mental. Some are financial while others are relational. Whatever the situation, there is no battle God cannot win. As for us, if we'll follow the four-step plan God has set forth, we'll experience victory every time. Wait on God. Watch Him work. Worry not about the outcome. And worship the One Who fights all our battles.

The enemy is drawing near. Is your battle plan in place?

RISE UP AND BUILD

WHY WE SHOULDN'T TRUST OUR FEELINGS

Making the transition to a healthier lifestyle is hard work! It's not about the deprivation or having to give up some of my favorite things, though I'll admit that was difficult during the first couple of weeks. It's the roller coaster ride of detoxing and cleansing that is necessary to get the body where it needs to be.

I've been working towards a healthier me for several weeks now. The first week and a half were horrible. I craved everything in sight. My head ached so badly from caffeine and sugar withdrawal that I thought I'd go crazy. Every muscle in my body seemed to hurt, and I was so very tired. Still, day after day, I'd tell myself, "Don't cheat. Keep going. Keep doing the right things. In just a few more days you'll be on the other side of this, and you'll feel so much better. Don't give in, Dana. You can do it."

And I did, and you know what? On the other side of that initial detox and withdrawal, I did feel so much better. I awoke in the mornings refreshed and renewed. My attitude was brighter. There was a spring in my step. The headaches had gone. The body aches were only those that resulted from the exercise my body was unused to. Above all, I was happy. For the first time in a long time, I felt good. Not only that, but I lost four pounds. Awesome!

Unfortunately, at the end of last week, I hit the next wave of detox. You see, the first detox was my body ridding itself of the toxins that were simply floating around in my system. Because I've been eating so healthy and exercising regularly for the past few weeks, my body has begun to burn fat, which is good and bad. Good because that's what I want it to do. Bad because toxins are stored in fat, and when the body burns off the fat, all those toxins are released into the body, which again tries to rid itself of these negative substances. In other words, detox round two.

For the past several days, I've felt horrible again. The headaches and body aches are back. My stomach has been alternating between queasy and crampy. Two of the four pounds that I lost reappeared. But the worst of it is that my attitude and outlook have gone south big time! I mean, seriously, I was working so hard and making so much progress only to feel as bad or worse now as I did before I began. And I admit, I had myself questioning whether it was really worth it. My feelings were telling me it was time to quit and to comfort myself with a huge piece of chocolate cake which I could wash down with a nice refreshing Pepsi.

I felt bad. I felt discouraged and frustrated. I felt like all my effort had been in vain. But while those feelings were very real, they weren't all true. That stretch between my first and second detox showed me that I'm on the right track. It gave me a sneak peak at what is awaiting me once I finally get myself back in shape. It showed me that my efforts have not been in vain. The healthy lifestyle is working, and my body—though currently making me miserable—is doing what it's supposed to do. It's getting rid of the bad in order to make room for the good.

So, you see, while my feelings said that it wasn't worth it, that's not true. I simply haven't reached my final destination yet, and I can't abort the entire journey based on one stretch of bumpy roads. Besides, I've come too far to turn back now. I've already made it through the first round of detox, and from the way I'm feeling today, I think I'm nearing the end of the second. If I stop now, I'll only have to go through all of that again, the next time I try to embark on a new journey toward better health. I don't want to retrace those steps. They were difficult enough the first time. No, I'm in this race until the end, and I'm happy to say that the Lord has helped me through this. Despite feeling bad, I was able to continue my daily exercise and my new healthy eating patterns.

Have you ever put your all into something only to be met with disappointment or frustration? Ever asked yourself, "Why bother?" If so, then dear friend, I urge you to finish out this journey. Don't stop now. Your efforts are not in vain, and things will work out as they should in the end. Just remember, this isn't the end yet. Keep doing those things you know you should do, and do them with a smile, knowing that your reward is soon to come. Hang in there, and whatever you do, don't trust your feelings. They can definitely lead us astray.

Therefore, my beloved brethren, be ye stedfast, unmoveable, always abounding in the work of the Lord, forasmuch as ye know that your labour is not in vain in the Lord.
I Corinthians 15:58

TO GO OR NOT TO GO?—THAT IS THE QUESTION

The book of Jeremiah paints a vivid picture of a terrible time for Israel. They were backslidden and hard-hearted, and despite Jeremiah's numerous attempts to convey the Lord's wishes for reconciliation, the nation would not have it. They were content in their wicked ways. . .until, that is, God's punishment fell upon them. As He had declared He would do, He allowed the nation to be taken over by the king of Babylon. Most of Israel was taken captive, but a few were left behind to tend the fields.

Over time, more and more refugees found their way to Judah where the king of Babylon had set up an overseer to rule the people. The prophet Jeremiah was among those in this camp, but though they were not captives in Babylon, their lives were far from easy, especially after their leader was killed. In a panic, the people sought to flee to Egypt, but before going, they asked Jeremiah to seek the Lord's will. Look what they had to say:

Then they said to Jeremiah, The Lord be a true and faithful witness between us, if we do not even according to all things for the which the Lord thy God shall send thee to us. Whether it be good, or whether it be evil, we will obey the voice of the Lord our God, to whom we send thee; that it may be well with us, when we obey the voice of the Lord our God. (Jeremiah 42:5-6)

After ten days, the Lord gave Jeremiah the directions he had been seeking. He basically told the people to stay put. He promised them if they would stay where they were, He would set everything straight. He would return them and all that they had to their rightful land. They need not fear the king of Babylon any longer. If they would just hold out and stay put, God promised to meet all their needs and more.

On the other hand, if they went to Egypt, God assured them that they would all die. Take a look:

But if ye say, We will not dwell in this land, neither obey the voice of the Lord your God, Saying, No; but we will go into the land of Egypt, where we shall see no war, nor hear the sound of the trumpet, nor have hunger of bread; and there will we dwell: And now therefore hear the word of the Lord, ye remnant of Judah; Thus saith the Lord of hosts, the God of Israel; If ye wholly set your faces to enter into Egypt, and go to sojourn there; Then it shall come to pass, that the sword, which ye feared, shall over-take you there in the land of Egypt, and the famine, whereof ye were afraid, shall follow close after you there in Egypt; and there ye shall die. So shall it be with all the men that set their faces to go into Egypt to sojourn there; they shall die by the sword, by the famine, and by the pestilence: and none of them shall remain or escape from the evil that I will bring upon them.   (Jeremiah 42:13-17)

Pretty clear answer, huh?   So what did Israel do? *Then spake Azariah the son of Hoshaiah, and Johanan the son of Kareah, and all the proud men, saying unto Jeremiah, Thou speakest falsely: the Lord our God hath not sent thee to say, Go not into Egypt to sojourn there. . .So they came into the land of Egypt: for they obeyed not the voice of the Lord: thus came they even to Tahpanhes. - Jeremiah 42:2,7*

So much for following the Lord! I could say a lot about that right now, but for the sake of time, I'm going to move on to the main thought that the Lord impressed on me this morning.

Without doing any harm to the Scriptures, I would like to share with you the interpretation of God's command that came to my mind upon reading it. "Child, I know you're tired and you're scared, but I have you where you are for a purpose. If you'll just be still and stay where I've placed you, I will set everything straight. You don't need to fear. I will save you. I will deliver you. I will show you mercy upon mercies. Stay and be blessed. However, if you're determined to go your own way and do your own thing, I won't stop you. But know this: when you're outside of my will, there will be consequences, and they will be severe. I know it looks better over there right now, but I promise you, it's not what it seems, and you will come to regret it later. Trust me, child. You're better off where you are, safe and secure in my will. Won't you stay with me?"

Stay or go? The choice is yours, but I warn you, anytime we stray outside of God's will, we'll wish we hadn't. Follow God's leading even when the path looks grim, for He has promised there's a brighter day coming!

RISE UP AND BUILD

WHEN GOD'S WAYS SEEM CRAZY

Last weekend, Jason and I visited the Battlefield of Cowpens for a Revolutionary War weekend. It was a very educational and exciting trip and served as research for one of my upcoming books. Since I've lived in South Carolina most of my life, one would think I would have visited the site by now or would have at least been more familiar with this part of the Revolutionary War, but sad to say, I was ignorant.

What I discovered is that the Battle of Cowpens was a turning point in the Revolutionary War and brought hope to the South who had faced multiple defeats. The odd thing is that this victory came about because of two men who were willing to set aside logic and do what they thought was best. It was their unconventional orders that led to a battle that was won in less than an hour.

First off, there was General Nathanael Greene, the leader in charge of the southern troops. At the time, he was stationed in Virginia, trying to prevent the advancement of the British troops into the North. Knowing his troops were outnumbered and unprepared for a full-on assault, he made the bold decision to split his army in half, hoping to force the British to do the same. Led by Daniel Morgan, a portion of Greene's army made their way into the upstate of South Carolina. Greene's plan worked, and the British divided their army, sending a portion to meet Morgan in Cowpens.

Daniel Morgan is known today as a tactical genius. Despite having the advantage of choosing his battleground, Morgan opted to fight in an open wood. He formed his troops in three lines straddling the road. The frontline was a small group of sharpshooters who were given the task to slow the British advance with well-aimed fire, then fall back. Ninety yards behind them was Andrew Pickens' regional militia. After two volleys of gunfire at killing distance, they were to fall behind the Continentals. Another 150 yards behind them were 600 crack militia Continentals from Maryland, Delaware and Virginia, who had orders to protect the militia and to be ready to fight.

Both of these men employed methods that were unorthodox and questionable, and no doubt, some of their men were scratching their heads and wondering if they should follow such ludicrous commands. I'm reminded of Joshua and his army when the Lord commanded them to march around the walls of Jericho for seven days. What kind of battle plan was that? Or how about Gideon, when God continued to whittle his army down until he was left with only 300 men? His army was outnumbered 450 to 1. Horrible odds, right?

But we can relate, can't we? I think we can all remember back to a time when God asked us to do something that made absolutely no sense, at least not in our minds. Perhaps it was the time He asked us to give money when we had none to give. Or maybe it was the time He asked us to leave a paying job for one that guaranteed nothing in return. Whatever the situation, God gave the command that seemed ludicrous, unconventional and downright scary. The question is, what did you do? What would you do if God asked you again?

The Lord has given us proof time and again that, even though His ways are not our ways, they are best and they are productive. Whether it be a battle against enemy soldiers or one against negative thoughts and feelings, we can always trust that God's ways are the right ways, even when they don't make sense. God has proven Himself faithful, and He has shown us that his methods—though unconventional

—produce results. Our job is not to question or to try to make sense of the process. Our only job is to obey. God will take care of the rest.

For what man knoweth the things of a man, save the spirit of man which is in him? even so the things of God knoweth no man, but the Spirit of God.
I Corinthians 2:11

RISE UP AND BUILD

HANG ON A LITTLE LONGER

The other night I decided to fix a big pot of chicken and dumplings. My dogs, Mitchell and Tippy, were all for this idea. They understood that the big bag of leftover chicken meant they could have a few samples. What they didn't understand, however, was that the chicken was the last thing to go in the pot. First, there would be a lot of waiting as the dumplings cooked.

Mitchell quickly realized that the process was going to be a long one, so he went and made himself comfortable on the couch. Tippy, on the other hand, was determined to wait it out. So, she waited while the water boiled. She waited while the dumplings were added. She waited as I unloaded and loaded the dishwasher while the dumplings were cooking. She waited while I checked to see if the dumplings were done. Patient as ever, she sat behind me and waited.

After seeing that the dumplings needed a few more minutes before I added the chicken, I went into my office to do a quick task that I had forgotten about until then. Unfortunately, Tippy misunderstood my actions and obviously assumed that the "chicken feast" was a bust. When I went back to the kitchen, she was gone. As I opened the bag of chicken, Mitchell came running, but Tippy was still nowhere to be found. As I added the meat to the pot and tossed bits and pieces to Mitchell, Tippy was still AWOL. Finally, just as I was about to add the last of the chicken, she came in through the back door. Fortunately for her, I had been saving some scraps.

Funny, isn't it? She waited all that time, then just about the time she was going to get her reward, she gave up and wandered off. . . and nearly missed the reward because of it. Sounds familiar, doesn't it? Look at the passage I read in my devotions this morning: *Oh that my people had hear-kened unto me, and Israel had walked in my ways! I should soon have subdued their en-emies, and turned my hand against their ad-versaries. The haters of the Lord should have submitted themselves unto him: but their time should have endured for ever. He should have fed them also with the finest of the wheat: and with honey out of the rock should I have satisfied thee. (Psalm 81:13-16)*

Did you catch that phrase, "I should soon have subdued their enemies"? God was saying, "I was about to give them what they wanted. I was about to make their dreams come true. I was about to bring all my promises to fruition. But Israel wouldn't wait any longer." No, they grew tired of wait-ing on God and decided to do things their own way. If only they had waited just a little while longer!

I don't want to be like the children of Israel. I don't want to be like Tippy. I don't want to miss out on the blessings of God because I gave up one hour, one day, or even one year too early. I want all the things God has promised me and all the blessings that He has in store for me, but in order to have them, I need to be patient throughout the entire process. Yes, it may seem like nothing is happening, but God is always working.

Maybe today you're about ready to give up. I urge you to hold on a little longer. God has a treat in store for you. Don't wander off. Stay in His presence, and wait on His timing. I promise you the blessings He has for you will definitely be worth it (and they may or may not taste like chicken).

MAJORING IN THE MINOR

I love minor keys. I love to hear them. I love to play them. There's just something about them that is beautiful to my ears, and yet there is also a sadness in their melody. For all their beauty, they are solemn and almost mournful. Strangely enough, the feelings evoked in me are not those of sadness but those of peace and serenity. Pieces played in the minor tend to set my mind at ease and help me to find rest for my weary soul.

I have heard minor keys referred to as the tragedies of life and major keys as the triumphs of life. But I ask you this: how can one have triumph without first having tragedy? It is not possible for one to be victorious without first fighting a battle. For one to be an overcomer, he or she must face struggles. And while one can play in a major key without using the minor keys, is the melody as sweet?

I shudder to think of all the classics that would be lost if we were to throw out all music with minor keys. To do so would be simply insane. Yet why do we often insist that God remove the minor keys from our lives? Why do we plead with Him to remove the battles through which we gain our victories? Why do we implore Him to remove our tragedies thus also removing our triumphs? Why can't we simply leave the music alone?

Life is full of music, but it takes both major and minor keys for us to fully appreciate either one. Do not fear the mournful tones or the solemn silence between the notes. Instead, find peace and serenity in the flow of the music, knowing that the Master Musician is planning a grand finale that will take your breath away.

But the God of all grace, who hath called us unto his eternal glory by Christ Jesus, after that ye have suffered a while, make you perfect, stablish, strengthen, settle you.
I Peter 5:10

RISE UP AND BUILD

THE PIT OF VOICES

*He brought me up also out of an horrible pit,
out of the miry clay, and set my feet upon a
rock, and established my goings.
Psalm 40:2*

I believe all Christians can relate to this verse in one form or another. How many times has God delivered us from danger? How many times has He led us where we needed to go? While there's loads of good meat in this one verse alone, I want to focus on the phrase "an horrible pit".

Have you ever felt like you were in a pit and no matter how hard you struggled, you just couldn't get out? Maybe it was a pit of despair. Or perhaps it was a pit of loneliness. A pit of depression or a pit of fatigue. I think we would all agree that those are horrible pits to find oneself in. But the pit to which David is referring here is even worse.

In the Hebrew, the phrase "an horrible pit" is translated as "pit of voices." Unfortunately, we can relate to that pit as well.

The world cries out to us, "Have it your way!" Satan whispers in our ears, "Hath God said. . .?" Even our own flesh calls out, "Life is hard. I deserve a little happiness, don't I?" And somewhere amid the cacophony is the still, small voice of the Savior saying, "Child, follow my lead."

We used to play a game with our church youth group that illustrated this pit of voices rather well. Each team was made up of two players. One player traversed an obstacle course while blindfolded, and the other gave the teammate directions. The trick was that every other team was allowed to speak to the obstacle-facing contestant, and of course, they often chose to shout out incorrect directions meant to confuse, overwhelm and lead astray. The only way the player could be successful was if he/she drowned out all other voices except that of his/her teammate.

Sometimes in life, I feel like I'm a contestant in this game without even realizing it. Just like the player, friend and foe alike are filling my ears with advice, direction and suggestions. It's up to me to filter out all other noise and to listen intently for that still, small voice. Only then will I successfully finish the course.

RISE UP AND BUILD

ACTIVATE YOUR FAITH

Activate your faith. What a simple, yet profound statement. I heard it proclaimed yesterday at a ladies' meeting. The speaker spoke of how the phrase changed her life, and in the moments after she said it, I realized it was going to change mine as well.

I had always compared my faith to an automatic function like that of the adrenal gland. The adrenal gland is the part of the body that senses danger or excitement and automatically activates to send the body into "fight or flight" mode. You know—adrenaline rush. This process is not something we have to think about. When being confronted by a frightening situation, we don't have to tell our hearts to beat faster. It just happens. It's a reaction. It works the way God intended for it to work. It's our bodies' automatic response.

Faith is not like that at all, and until yesterday, I hadn't really thought about it. To be honest, I've often felt that I must be the lousiest believer on the planet because every time stormy circumstances come my way, I find myself running for cover instead of braving the winds. Faith? What faith? Why can't I be like Paul who boldly said, "Infirmities. Persecutions. Trials. Bring it on. It's no big deal"? What? Are you insane? Of course it's a big deal.

But now I understand the difference between Paul and myself. Paul activated his faith; I've merely been waiting for mine to automatically kick in. It just doesn't work that way. Activating our faith takes time, effort and a willingness to be uncomfortable for a little while. Activating our faith requires us to study, memorize and claim God's promises. It requires us to be on guard against the deadly darts of the devil such as destructive thoughts and attitudes, "little sins," and feelings of envy or bitterness. It requires a conscious decision of "No, I will not give in. No, I'm not running this time." And it requires us to give up the reins. We must stop trying to live our lives by our plans and agendas, and must instead completely surrender to God. (I never said this would be easy!)

Activate your faith. It doesn't work on auto-pilot. And the process will not be an easy one. But I guarantee you this: it will be rewarding!

But without faith it is impossible to please him: for he that cometh to God must believe that he is, and that he is a rewarder of them that diligently seek him.
Hebrews 11:6

RISE UP AND BUILD

WHEN IT SEEMS THERE IS NO HOPE

Thou art wearied in the greatness of thy way; yet saidst thou not, There is no hope: thou hast found the life of thine hand; therefore thou wast not grieved.
Isaiah 57:10

During my Bible reading last week, this verse jumped out at me, and today I would like to make an application using this verse. Let's begin with the first phrase: *Thou art wearied in the greatness of thy way.* Does the way before you seem great today? Does the path appear long and scary? Troublesome roads can leave us weary, even if we haven't traveled them yet. Just the thought of the path ahead is enough to cause fear and dread. Whether were facing a difficult day, week or even year, the path before us evokes anxiety within us, making us weary before even taking the first step.

But look at the next phrase in this verse in Isaiah: *yet saidst thou not, There is no hope.* No matter how tired, weary or fearful we may become, we should never allow ourselves to feel that there is no hope. There is always hope. Jesus made sure of that when He came to die and rise again. Not only did He purchase our salvation, but He also bought our right to believe and have faith in the things we cannot see, including the things that lie at the end of the road we are facing. And as long as Jesus lives, there will be hope.

So how can we tap into that hope? In the midst of our dread and anxiety, how can we remember that God will get us through this? The answer can be found in the very next phrase of the verse above: *thou hast found the life of thine hand; therefore thou wast not grieved.* To dispel the fear and worry, we must remember who life is all about and in whose hand our lives are held. Psalm 27:1 says, *The Lord is my light and my salvation; whom shall I fear? the Lord is the strength of my life; of whom shall I be afraid?* The Lord is the strength of my life; therefore, I need not fear anyone or anything. The Bible assures me that He will never leave me nor forsake me, and because of that, I should not lose hope. If the Lord is with me, there is nothing I cannot do.

I do not know what road or situation you are facing today, but I urge you to remember these words. Don't lose hope, dear friend. God will get you through this, no matter how impossible it seems. He is walking with you, and His loving arms of protection surround you. Though the way before you may seem daunting, go forward in faith, knowing that the Lord is the strength of your life, and because of that, you can continue to walk in hope.

In Christ, there is no such thing as a hopeless situation!

FEAR NOT TOMORROW

The entire chapter of Exodus 16 is devoted to the first instance of manna for the children of Israel. And while there is much we can learn from manna, I would like to focus on a few things the Lord brought to my attention in my recent studies. These things have been a blessing to me, and I hope they will be an encouragement to you as well.

The first lesson I see from manna is that we need to focus on today, not yesterday or tomorrow. To quote from the movie **Kung Fu Panda**, "Yesterday is history. Tomorrow is a mystery, but today is a gift. That is why we call it the present." Though this saying is from a cartoon movie, there is much wisdom in it. On more than one occasion, the Bible reminds us to keep our focus on today rather than yesterday or tomorrow, and that is precisely what we learn from Exodus 16 as well.

Then said the Lord unto Moses, Behold, I will rain bread from heaven for you; and the people shall go out and gather a certain rate every day, that I may prove them, whether they will walk in my law, or no. - Exodus 16:4

As he promised, God rained down manna from heaven every day except the Sabbath. The people were instructed to gather what they needed for the day, no more and no less. If they tried to hoard manna for the next day, it spoiled and became infested with maggots. In a sense, God was showing his people that He would provide for them each day, every day and that they could trust Him to provide for their needs.

In Matthew six, when Jesus is teaching the disciples how to pray, He uses this phrase: *Give us this day our daily bread.*

Did you catch that? He prayed for daily bread, not weekly, monthly or yearly. No, He prayed that His needs for the day would be met and instructed the disciples to pray in the same way. Later on, in the same chapter, the Bible instructs us, *Take therefore no thought for the morrow: for the morrow shall take thought for the things of itself. Sufficient unto the day is the evil thereof.* Don't worry about tomorrow. God is already there, and He has already set things in order for us. We don't need to fret about it or spend today's strength and energy worrying about it.

I often wonder how much better I would feel, how much more energy I would have, and how much less anxiety I would have if I were to live one day at a time instead of regretting past mistakes and fretting over future events. What would happen if I used the grace, strength and provision that God gave me each day to live out that day and that day only? I can't help but think I would be more focused, more productive and more joyful.

Please understand, there's nothing wrong with making plans or having a daily schedule, but there is everything wrong with living in the past and dreading the future. The psalmist tells us that this is the day the Lord has made, and we are to rejoice and be glad in it. We're not even promised a to-morrow. The Lord may take us home before it comes, so why waste today's time and strength worrying about something that may never be? Instead, let us trust that God is al-ready there, that He is working all things for our good and that we can trust in His never-ending faithfulness. Then, let us live this day to its fullest, leaving the past behind us and the future in God's hands.

Just as the Lord promised, He rained down manna from heaven six days a week, every week for forty years. The children of Israel never went without. There was always enough, and they never had to worry about their next meal. God proved his faithfulness to them, and that God is the same God we serve. He has promised to provide for our needs, and He will keep that promise. Trust in that and enjoy today!

RISE UP AND BUILD

CAUTION! TURNS AHEAD!

Sometimes we come to life's crossroads
and view what we think is the end,
But God has a much wider vision,
and He knows it's only a bend.
The road will go on and get smoother,
and after we've stopped for a rest,
The path that lies hidden beyond us
is often the part that is best.
So rest and relax and grow stronger;
let go and let God share your load,
And have faith in a brighter tomorrow;
you've just come to a bend in the road.
Helen Steiner Rice

A bend in the road. Scary thought, isn't it? I mean the road has been rough enough, but now there's a bend too? A bend that we can't see beyond. A bend that could be hiding any number of possibilities from

129

our view. A bend that could change everything, and let's face it—change frightens us.

I'm reminded of a roller coaster. I love the crazy things. Big hills? Bring it on. Twisty turns? That's the way I like it. Corkscrew loops? Oh, yeah! Pitch black? Um, now wait a minute. Yes, you've discovered my weakness—I'm scared of the dark. Well, not really, but a roller coaster I would enjoy in the light has the tendency to bring me to the brink of terror in the dark. I don't mind the hills, the corkscrews, the twists and the turns. . .as long as I know they're coming. In the darkness, I can't see, so I don't know what to expect. And somehow, that uneasiness of the unknown turns my adrenalin rush into genuine fear.

The unknown has a way of doing that. That's why those bends in the road cause such anxiety. But could it be that we're missing something? Could it be that we're so worked up about the unknown and the path that is hidden from view that we're missing one of the biggest results of a bend in the road? We know that God has a purpose for everything. He doesn't place bends in the road for no reason, and I think one of those reasons is to make us slow down.

Think about it, when we're driving and we come up to a bend in the road, what do we do? We hit the brakes, right? Most of us (and I say "most" because I've seen some drivers that might not qualify for this statement) wouldn't dream of hitting that bend at our current speed. That speed is meant for straightaways, not for curves. So, out of good sense and a desire to stay safe, we slow down and take the bend at a reduced speed.

Perhaps that is all God is trying to do with our current bends in the road. He wants us to slow down. He desires for us to be still. He longs for us to take some time to just be. It is during those times that we can feel His closeness and hear His voice. How many times have we missed it because there's too much to do, because we were simply speeding through life?

A few weeks ago, I started the routine of taking an afternoon nap. I know it sounds crazy, but I was tired of feeling like a hamster on a wheel. I was exhausted and overwhelmed. Too much to do, not enough time and energy to get it all done. You know the routine, right? At first, I argued that I couldn't give up an hour of my time each day. I already wasn't getting everything done. I also argued that I don't like naps and that I would never be able to sleep in the middle of the afternoon.

Well, so far, I haven't slept during a single nap, but I have gotten still, and in that stillness each day, I've felt my joy and peace being restored. So much so that I was much more happy and productive in the afternoon than I had been before I started napping. There's just something about getting the body (and the mind) still for a while, and honestly, I think far too many of us are racing around the curves instead of using those bends in the road as a sign to slow down.

I know there's a lot to do. Trust me, I understand. But may I remind you that "Be still and know that I am God" is not a request or suggestion? It's a command. How many of us are heeding it?

Are you facing a bend in the road? Is that sense of uneasiness getting out of control? Take it easy. God is working all things for your good, so whatever is waiting around the bend is a good thing. In the meantime, slow down and enjoy the ride. After all, the Driver has it under control.

Be still, and know that I am God: I will be
exalted among the heathen,
I will be exalted in the earth.
Psalm 46:10

THE POWER OF A LITTLE THING

As I've mentioned before, I am not a coffee drinker. I love the smell of it, but I can't stand the taste of the stuff, no matter how much milk or sugar I add. Yuck! I do, however, enjoy several cups of herbal tea throughout my day. And unlike most people, I create my own herbal tea concoctions. I buy a variety of tea bags at Bargain Foods where I can get boxes of 20-100 tea bags for anywhere from 89 cents to $2. Then I place a mix of tea bags in my "special" coffee pot (special, because it's only used for making tea), add some water, let it brew and enjoy my special blend all day long. My blends usually consists of two or more of the following: green tea, white tea, peppermint, chamomile, spearmint, lemon, honey, ginger, and vanilla. Sometimes I even blend teas that are already herbal blends. It just depends on my mood and whether I want a calming or invigorating tea.

Anyway, last night, Jason offered to make the tea and asked what I wanted. "Whatever you want to throw together," I commented, not taking into consideration that there was one particular tea in the pantry that did not mix well with some of the others. I remembered this fact as soon as I smelled the tea, but the damage had already been done. Just as I usually do, Jason had combined some mint teas with chamomile and lemon. Fine. Unfortunately, he had also thrown one bag of Vanilla Caramel in with the mix. Vanilla and mint are fine together, as are vanilla and chamomile. Vanilla and lemon is not my favorite blend, but it's not bad. However, the caramel doesn't really blend well with any of them, particularly the lemon and the mint.

The result was a smooth, yet strange-tasting, tea that left an indescribable taste in my mouth after I managed to down half the cup. Not wanting to hurt Jason's feelings, I did my best to drink it, but I just couldn't, and after he left for work this morning, I dumped the rest of it down the drain and started a new batch. I'm sorry. He meant well, and it was really my fault for not remembering about the Vanilla Caramel. Besides, the only way I knew how badly it blended with the other teas is because I had tried it before myself. . . and learned my lesson.

As I prepared my new batch of tea this morning, I was reminded of the phrase in the Bible: *a little leaven leaveneth the whole lump (Galatians 5:9, I Corinthians 5:6).* Oddly enough, I came across that same phrase when reading a devotional by a friend and fellow author, Lynn Mosher. I thought about how that one little tea bag made the entire pot of tea nearly undrink-able. There were probably eight to ten bags in that batch of tea, several of which were strong mint blends. Yet it was all overpowered by one little tea bag. And as a result, the entire pot was wasted. It was no good. I couldn't stomach it.

Sin is the same way. We often overlook what we call "the small sins." A little lie. A slight exaggeration. Going a few miles over the speed limit. Taking a little extra time on break at work. Forsaking our Bible reading and prayer time. They're not big sins like murder, adultery or thievery, so they're acceptable, right? I mean, we're only human, after all. We can't be expected to be perfect. We live in a sinful world and inhabit sinful bodies. Sin is just a part of life, right?

Unfortunately, yes, it is now a part of life, but that doesn't mean it's excusable or acceptable. It doesn't mean that God is not watching or that Jesus didn't have to die for those "little sins." What it does mean is that we need to be on guard. What starts out as a "little sin" may well become something much greater. Sin always leads to more sin! It's a never-ending process, and as soon as we become lax and allow things to slip by unnoticed, those "little sins" begin to grow and take on a life of their own.

One tea bag was enough to ruin an entire pot of tea. One sin is enough to ruin our relationship with the Father. I'm not talking about losing our salvation. That can't happen. Salvation is forever, and nothing can change that. But when we're living in sin, even "little sin," there is a wall separating us from God. It hinders our walk together and our communication with Him. It drives a wedge between us that only confession of that sin can remedy. And just as the tea left a sour taste in my mouth, don't you know our sin leaves a sour taste in God's?

I'll let you in on a little secret: there are no "little sins." They're all big to God. They all cost Him the life of His Son. And they are all signs of rebellion to His authority. Let's keep that in mind the next time we want to go a little faster than we should or take a longer break than we're allotted. Let's remember that fact when we allow our minds to wander where they shouldn't go and our mouths to say words they shouldn't utter. Sin is sin, and it is powerful. Just like the leaven. Just like the Vanilla Caramel tea. It can ruin and destroy, and I guarantee you the cost will be more than some funky-tasting tea.

DON'T BE AFRAID TO REWRITE YOUR STORY

I'm working on a new book, and I have to admit that, from the very beginning, this story has given me grief. In the beginning stages, I struggled with plot, characters, settings and how to weave each of these elements into a story of intrigue and excitement. For days, I struggled with writer's block, unable to write a single word to bring the story to life. I've written and published sixteen books, and this has never happened to me before.

Finally, after days of frustration, I began to write, and the words flowed from me. Though I was excited that the writer's block seemed to have been broken, I couldn't seem to get excited about the story itself. Still, I didn't want to lose my momentum, so I continued to write and to do my best to create a story that readers would love. Unfortunately, after I had written nearly two-thirds of the book, I realized that the story had taken a drastic turn, and I was not happy with the direction it was headed. The character development just wasn't there. The plot appeared stilted and forced. All in all, it seemed like the entire thing was a disaster!

After pouring out my feelings to Jason, he gave me some profound advice though it wasn't particularly what I wanted to hear at that moment. His words to me were this: "Don't be afraid to rewrite your story." The truth is, I'm not afraid, but I am frustrated. I don't want to rewrite my book. I don't want all of the work I've already done to be in vain. I hate the thought of starting all over again and possibly discovering that the story still doesn't work. So, I guess I am afraid—afraid of failing again.

Perhaps you know exactly how I feel. No, you may not be writing a physical novel, but you are writing your own life story. And maybe that story has taken a drastic turn, and you're not happy with where it is heading. Like me, you may have struggled with writer's block, unable to tell your story. But then, one day, Jesus came into your life, and your story began to flow like never before. You were excited and had high expectations of how your story would play out, but then, you realized your story was heading in a new direction, and you were not happy with the results.

It is to you I say, don't be afraid to rewrite your story. Yes, I know there are some things in your past that cannot be changed and even some things in your present that cannot be altered, just as there are some elements in my story that cannot be rewritten. There are things that were set in motion in the previous books, and now I must follow through with them. But that is not to say we cannot retrace our steps and discover where our story took a wrong turn. I still have to discover where that point is in my book, but looking back on my own life, I now see that my life lost its direction when I allowed fear to replace my faith. Knowing that, I can go back to that place and begin a new story— one built on faith in my God who has always met my needs and will continue to meet my needs.

Here's the tough part. It's not enough to simply want to go back and rewrite our stories; we must be willing to allow the stories to play out the way God sees fit, not the way we expect them to play out. I have been trying to force my book to play out the way I wanted instead of allowing it to go where it needed to go. And in that, I've made a mess.

So, you see, the truth is we are not the ones rewriting our stories after all. We are handing our pen to the Author and Finisher of our faith and allowing him to write our story as He deems worthy. I'm not saying it will be easy or that it will be painless, but isn't a good story worth it?

Now, if you'll excuse me, I have some rewriting to do!

Therefore if any man be in Christ, he is a new creature: old things are passed away; behold, all things are become new.
II Corinthians 5:17

RISE UP AND BUILD

WILL I EVER GRADUATE FROM THIS CLASS?

With Jason working split shifts again, my mood has gradually shifted into a state of discontentment. I've found myself whining, "Not this again. Sure, the paychecks are nice, but is it worth it if both of us are tired and grouchy from lack of sleep?" Of course, my rants don't stop with that one complaint. Before long, I'm fussing about my aching shoulder, the firewood that needs to be split, Tippy's incessant scratching because of her skin problem, people's unfair expectations of me because I don't have a "real job" and on the list goes. Let me tell you, you don't want to be anywhere around when this pity party is taking place. It's ugly!

As I prayed this morning, the Lord brought a verse to my mind—a verse, in fact, that the preacher had spoken about Wednesday night at church. Coincidence? I think not. Philippians 4:11 states, *Not that I speak in respect of want: for I have learned, in whatsoever state I am, therewith to be content.* I've heard, read and quoted this verse so many times, but just recently I realized that I was missing a big piece of the puzzle. All this time, I believed Paul was content because it was in his nature or maybe because of some supernatural power bestowed upon him by God. The way he could suffer all that he suffered and still walk away saying, "I'm content" had to be some sort of miracle, right?

Well, yes and no. The fact of the matter is that Paul's contentment was the result of his education. Notice he didn't say, "I am content." No, he said, "I *have learned* to be content." It wasn't an automatic thing for Paul any more that it is an automatic thing for me. Paul didn't just sit down one day and decide that he was going to be content with whatever life threw his way. His pursuit of contentment was a process. It was an ongoing battle, day after day, situation after situation, until he finally got to the point where he could honestly say, "Okay, now I'm content." It didn't happen overnight.

Another sobering fact is that this education took place, not in a classroom, but through the trials of life. Each event in his ministry was a lesson that he took to heart. "Circumstances are bad, but God still delivers. Some people absolutely hate me, but God will always love me. I have no idea what the future holds, but I know the One who holds the future. God will supply everything I need; everything else will just be a hindrance to my calling." See what I mean? Every message he preached, every beating he received, the shipwrecks, the imprisonments—they all instructed Paul in what it takes to be content. He learned through his trials, and because of that, he grew to the place where he could be content in the midst of his trials.

At this point in my life, I can honestly say, "I have learned, in whatsoever state I am, I *should be* content." To go beyond that, well, I guess I'm still learning. But I have been reminded that instead of complaining about my current trials, I should be thankful for the education I'm receiving. Through these tough times, God is teaching me to be content. Is He possibly doing the same for you?

TRICKLES OF BLESSING?

Yesterday, poor Jason's shower was a mere trickle. That happens from time to time in our bathroom. Dirt and debris build up in the filter of the shower head and eventually block the water flow. Jason was less than thrilled with his mediocre shower and immediately asked me if I had noticed the water pressure in the shower steadily decreasing. I had to be honest. "No, I can't say that I've noticed." (I promise you, I hadn't!)

Jason gathered up the appropriate tools and immediately went to work. He took apart the shower head and removed the filter. Sure enough, that thing was clogged big time! No wonder he couldn't get any water flow. After cleaning the filter, he put the shower head together again and instructed me to let him know if I noticed a difference when I got my shower. Boy, did I!

I would not be exaggerating in telling you that the water nearly knocked me down. I wasn't expecting so much force from my little shower head. How had I not noticed how much the water pressure had changed over time? How was it that I hadn't missed the exquisite nature of a shower that pounds on the body like a thousand tiny hammers? It was the best shower I had had in a long time, and I didn't want to leave. (In fact, I'm thinking about getting another one right now. Oh yeah! Well, maybe I'll finish this devotion first, but then. . .)

I think the reason I didn't notice the diminishing water pressure was because it happened so gradually. Day after day, the filter became a little more clogged, then a little more, then a little more. It happened so slowly that I never realized that anything had changed, but once Jason cleaned out that filter, whoa, what a difference!

The same thing can happen in our hearts. Little by little, they become clogged and weighed down by the dirt and debris of this world. Things like resentment, anger, and discontentment can gradually block the flow of love, mercy, and forgiveness. Like my shower, the blockage doesn't happen all at once. Instead, it builds slowly over time, allowing the heart to become more and more congested without our ever realizing it.

Fortunately, there is a cure, and as strange as it may sound, it is the same remedy that unclogged my shower head—someone needs to clean out the filter. In the case of my shower, that "someone" was Jason (like I would know how to do it!). In the case of our hearts, that "someone" is Christ. When we confess our sins, He will cleanse us of all unrighteousness (I John 1:9). He alone has what it takes to remove the resentment, anger, and discontentment from our hearts, and once He does, boy, will we notice a difference!

I wish I could tell you that, like salvation, this cleansing is a one-time fix, but alas, that is not the case. No, if we're not paying attention, our hearts will become clogged once again, just like my showerhead. But we can prevent (or at least lessen) this problem with a simple, heartfelt prayer found in the Psalms: *Search me, O God, and know my heart: try me, and know my thoughts: And see if there be any wicked way in me, and lead me in the way everlasting. (Psalm 139:23-24)*

Now that I realize, once again, how awesome my shower can feel, I don't want to let it get clogged up again. I would miss far too many great showers. It's not worth it! I can say the same for my heart. I don't want to miss out on the best that God has for me because my heart is too blocked by gunk to allow His spirit to flow freely as it should.

Showers of blessing or trickles of blessing? The choice is ours.

Lord, please search my heart and point out anything that I need to get right with you. Help me to empty my heart of anything that will hinder my walk with You, and lead me in the way that You have prepared for me. Amen!

RISE UP AND BUILD

WHEN GOOD TIMES ARE FORGOTTEN

Have you ever been in a valley so long and so dark that you eventually forgot all the good in your life? You didn't mean for it to happen. In fact, you didn't even realize it was happening until one day you examined your life and said, "This is my life. This is how it's always been, and I guess this is how it will always be." The happy times aren't even a memory. The blessings can't be remembered. It seems like the length and severity of the valley have cast a shadow over the good times that once were. In a sense, you find yourself in a famine. . . not of food, but of hope.

Behold, there come seven years of great plenty throughout all the land of Egypt: And there shall arise after them seven years of famine; and all the plenty shall be forgotten in the land of Egypt; and the famine shall consume the land; And the plenty shall not be known in the land by reason of that famine following; for it shall be very grievous. - Genesis 41:29-31

The above passage takes place during Joseph's captivity in Egypt. Temporarily free of his prison bonds, the young foreigner interprets Pharoah's dreams, informing the ruler that the kingdom would experience seven years of plenty followed by seven years of famine. He goes on to warn that the famine would be so severe that the plenty would be forgotten.

Strange, isn't it? Seven years of plenty. Seven years of famine. Seven years is seven years, right? So how can one time period wipe out the memory of the other? If you've ever been in a valley that seemed to stretch on for years, you'd understand the answer to that question. Seven years of plenty seems like a drop in a bucket compared to seven years of famine. Why? Because we have a tendency to take our blessings for granted. We expect life to treat us well. We expect to have our needs met. We expect God to bless us. And when He does, we briefly acknowledge it (if that) and then continue on our way.

When life isn't so kind, however, we tend to keep count of all that's gone wrong. We tally the injustices. We log the times when God could have intervened but seemed nowhere to be found. We chart the slight rise and continuous fall of our spirit and find ourselves asking, "God, how long will this last?"

I'm curious at what point during the seven years of famine the people forgot all about the time when they had plenty. One year? Halfway? I doubt it was the entire seven years though that's not to say it didn't feel like it. Yes, famines have a way of making time stand still, at least that's the way it seems to us. The good times, if we remember them at all, seem so far away, yet the famine appears to stretch on forever with no hope in sight. What can I say? That's the nature of famines.

We don't, however, do ourselves any favors by dwelling more on the negative than we do on the positive. Think about it for a moment. When we need something, how many hours do we spend praying for it? How many times do we ask God to grant our petition? How often do we ask others to help us pray about it? Then, when/if God does give us what we asked for, how do we respond? Do we spend as many hours thanking Him as we did asking for what we wanted? Do we continue to praise Him after the deed is done, or do we settle for a simple, "Thank you, Lord"? Do we tell others what God has done and invite them to join in our worship? Sometimes, maybe, but not usually. Is it any wonder, then, that the good times are forgotten so easily? If we don't spend time focusing on our blessings, they're very likely to be forgotten when tough times roll around.

Famine will come. It is inevitable. But we can be prepared. By focusing on our blessings and adopting an attitude of gratitude day after day, we can help our brains hold onto the good times even when things turn bad. Repetition aids learning, but it also supports memory. If we don't want to forget the good times, we need to rehearse them over and over again to keep them fresh in our minds.

How has God already blessed you? Think about it. Write it down. Praise the Lord for it. Tell others about it. Keep it fresh in your mind and in your heart. After all, it's hard to forget something that you're always thinking about.

RISE UP AND BUILD

WHAT'S WRONG WITH ME?

"What is wrong with me?"

It wasn't the first time I had asked myself this question, nor, I fear, will it be the last. Perhaps you can relate. Maybe you understand all too well what it's like to fall back into a bad habit or forbidden sin. If so, you can comprehend my frustration.

Last week was one of the best, most productive weeks I've had in a very long time. With wrapping up the ends of one book and beginning the planning process of another, I was full of motivation and passion for the work God has given me to do. Overall, my health cooperated and didn't hinder me from accomplishing my daily goals. My mind, though buzzing with ideas, felt free as a bird, uncluttered (for a change) by worry and anxiety. I felt close to the Lord as if He were literally walking by my side as I followed His will for my life. And even though I knew things were far from perfect in my life, I felt content.

And then the storm began. First, it was a letter bearing bad news. Drip! Then it was five (yes, five!) friends/family members who contacted me, asking for prayer about major issues they were struggling with in their lives. Drip, drip! Then there was the "in your face" reminder that Jason's weekly paycheck sported a whopping 25 hours. . . again! Boom!!!! And suddenly, I felt my happy little world crumble.

It wasn't the letter or the phone calls or the measly paycheck that rocked my world though they certainly didn't help. But rather, it was the result of those things. After a week or more of resting soundly in the grip of God's faithfulness, I felt the tug of anxiety on my soul. At first, it was a mere annoyance. But as the trials of the week grew, I found myself thinking less about God and more about my problems. My writing focus became more centered around profitability than on writing what God wanted me to write and leaving the results to Him. My mind, that only a few days before had been a placid pond, was now a roaring whirlpool of thoughts on how to "fix" things before they got any worse. And that's when I uttered the question I've become far too familiar with: "What is wrong with me?"

I had been making progress, finally leaving worry and anxiety in my wake. It hadn't been easy to make it so far, but the Lord helped me reach a new place in my spiritual walk, and I was happy there. And then I blew it! A few raindrops and claps of thunder sent me crawling back to my old ways, and when I realized how far I had fallen, I felt ashamed. And confused. Hasn't God proven Himself faithful to me time and again? Haven't we faced tougher situations than this? Didn't He always work it out somehow? Yes, yes, and yes! So, what's my problem? Why did I fall back to my old habit of worry? Why did I allow the storm to take away my serenity? What's wrong with me?

The same thing that's wrong with you. We're humans living in a fallen world. We're not perfect and never will be this side of Heaven. We mess up. We fall down. We fall back. But you know what? God knew all of this about us before He sent His Son to die for us. Before such a great sacrifice, God knew exactly who we would be and what we would do. He knew that we would fall. He even knew how often we would fall, yet He still loved us enough to offer His only begotten Son as a sacrifice for us. And as if that weren't enough (which it is), He promises to help us when we fall. He doesn't laugh at our misfortune. He doesn't shake His head and mutter, "What's wrong with you?" No, in love, He reaches down and lifts us from our self-made pit. Why? Because of a love so strong that it can never be broken, not even by our mistakes.

Whatever you've done, God still loves you. No matter how far you've strayed, He will take you back. He longs to lift you up, dust you off, and shower you with blessings of His love. Don't sit there pouting about your hard times or giving yourself a guilt trip about your recent slip-up. Get up. Get over it. And get back in God's will. I can't guarantee you things will be easy, but I can guarantee you that there will be peace and contentment. Who knows? Maybe you'll even find a bit of joy as you dance in the rain.

For I am persuaded, that neither death, nor life, nor angels, nor principalities, nor powers, nor things present, nor things to come, Nor height, nor depth, nor any other creature, shall be able to separate us from the love of God, which is in Christ Jesus our Lord.
Romans 8:38-39

CRYING ALONE IN THE DARK

Last weekend, while attending a church function, I was reminded just how important it is for us, as Christians, to bear one another's burdens. A friend and I were standing in the shade discussing the weather, the volleyball game taking place a few feet away, and other mundane things. Just your basic chit chat. Soon, however, my dear friend began to pour out her heart to me.

It seems she has been under a lot of stress lately, and I had no idea. She confessed to a spiritual battle taking place within her heart and mind and to having spells where all she could do is cry. As I listened, two thoughts came to my mind. First off, why hadn't I seen this? How could I have not noticed that one of my dearest friends was in such turmoil? Second, I thought of how I could totally relate to what she was saying because I had been going through the same thing. Though many of the circumstances surrounding our spiritual battles were different, some of them were the same. The more we talked, the more I realized that we had been experiencing the same feelings of frustration, discouragement, and utter fatigue. And we had both kept it to ourselves thinking no one else would understand or that others would think poorly of us if we admitted our feelings of total despair.

The rest of the weekend, I found myself wondering if my friend and I could have escaped some of the turmoil we had been through if we had only turned to someone for help. After all, I did feel better after having talked with her and realizing that I wasn't alone. It helped to talk to someone about my problems, but it also helped to hear that someone else was dealing with the same issues. It sounds strange, I know, but when she told me some of the things that she had been feeling, a wave of relief swept over me. I know this woman, and I hold her up as a beautiful example of what a Godly woman should be. To learn that she had the same feelings I did made me feel like less of a failure. Again, I know it sounds weird, but I think you understand what I'm saying.

I wonder how many of us go through our days and weeks crying alone in the dark because we fear that no one will understand or that people will judge us if they knew about the spiritual battle taking place deep within our hearts. Rather than taking the risk of exposing our faults and feelings, we keep them to ourselves and try to bear the burdens alone. But that's not how it should be. We need each other! God designed it that way from the very beginning. Remember, in the Garden of Eden, after God had created man, He said that it wasn't good for man to be alone. The Bible reinforces that fact many times, but none makes it clearer to me than Ecclesiastes 4:9-12, which says, *Two are better than one; because they have a good reward for their labour. For if they fall, the one will lift up his fellow: but woe to him that is alone when he falleth; for he hath not another to help him up. Again, if two lie together, then they have heat: but how can one be warm alone? And if one prevail against him, two shall withstand him; and a threefold cord is not quickly broken.*

Today, my friends, I want to make two things clear. First off, Christians do go through hard times. They get frustrated and can even suffer from depression. Knowing Christ does not exempt us from difficult circumstances or a lot of tears. Life is hard, and while faith in Christ does help us to get through, it doesn't mean that we don't experience times of discouragement and despair. Just as the psalmist, David.

Secondly, I want to remind you that there is strength and comfort in sharing our burdens with one another. We don't need to cry alone in the dark or hide our problems from others. True friends are there for one another in the good times and the bad. Reach out to them for help, and also pay attention to those around you and see if someone else needs to pour out their heart to you. Everyone is going through something, so let's make sure we're there for one another. It's easy to get so caught up in our own problems that we forget that others are hurting too. I'm reminded of a line from Mark Bishop's song, *Can I Pray for You?* which says, "Let me be there for you. We'll divide all your problems by two. And very soon there'll be three – you and Jesus and me. That's what friends are supposed to do."

You don't have to bear your burdens alone. None of us do! It's okay to cry, but please, don't cry alone.

RISE UP AND BUILD

ARE YOU GUARDING YOUR HEART?

In our ladies' Sunday School class, we've been talking about the armor of God. This past Sunday, our lesson was on the breastplate of righteousness. The breastplate protects the torso of the body, particularly the vital organs, including the heart. I think we all know and understand why it's important to protect our physical heart. After all, it controls the flow of blood in the body, and proper blood flow is essential for survival. But the question I want to pose to you today is this: Why is it important to guard our spiritual heart? I believe the Bible gives us three answers to that question.

1) Out of it are the issues of life.

Proverbs 4:23 says, *Keep thy heart with all diligence; for out of it are the issues of life.* So, what exactly does that mean? It means that our thoughts, actions, attitudes, and feelings are all dependent on the condition of our heart. A bitter heart leads to a bitter attitude, negative thoughts and feelings, and wrong actions. The same can be said of a hard heart or a resentful heart. Everything we are and everything we do is a reflection of what's in our heart. If we want a happy and peaceful life that is obedient to God, then we need to guard our heart against any influence that would destroy that happiness, peace or obedience.

2) It is the source of our words.

We often think of our brains as the source of our thoughts and words, but according to the Bible, that's not really the case. And if you think about it, I'm sure you'll agree that we've all said some things that seemed to bypass the brain before coming out of our mouths, right? Luke 6:45 reminds us, *A good man out of the good treasure of his heart bringeth forth that which is good; and an evil man out of the evil treasure of his heart bringeth forth that which is evil: for of the abundance of the heart his mouth speaketh.* The things that find their way into our hearts will eventually find their way out of our mouths. And we all know that once those hateful, bitter words have been spoken, we cannot take them back. The damage is done. Guarding our hearts is an essential part of making sure that we don't say things that we shouldn't say because the mouth will utter whatever the heart contains. A good heart equals good words. A bad heart? Well, you know the answer.

3) It is deceitful and desperately wicked.

It is imperative that we guard our hearts because they are naturally drawn to evil things. They cannot be trusted to do the right thing.   We learn this in Jeremiah 17:9 which says, *The heart is deceitful above all things, and desperately wicked: who can know it?* The heart wants what the heart wants whether it's a good thing or not. That is one reason I grow so aggravated when I hear someone giving the advice, "Well, you ought to just follow your heart." No, you shouldn't! Why would you follow something that God says is deceitful and desperately wicked? He goes on to say in Proverbs 28:26, *He that trusteth in his own heart is a fool. . .* Our hearts will lie to us. They will promise us great things, but in the end, all we will receive is disappointment and guilt. We must guard our hearts against outside evil influences and even from itself. Our hearts cannot be our guide through life. That's God's place.

Knowing this, is it any wonder God cautions us to daily take up our armor, including the breastplate of righteousness? The world is out to get us. Satan is out to destroy us. Even our own flesh is against us. Every day is a spiritual battle, and we must be armed and ready to defend ourselves and our faith. Guard your heart today, my friend!

RISE UP AND BUILD

IS GOD IN MY FAILURES?

A few years back, the Lord allowed us to get enough of a tax return to purchase our first full-size couch. In fact, we found an excellent deal on a sectional. It is a three-seat couch with a full-length chaise lounge attached to the end. As I type this devotion, Tippy is curled up at the far end of the couch, I am stretched out on the chaise, and Mitch is lying on the couch beside me with his head in my lap (a little tricky for typing, but hey!). If Jason were home, he could easily fit between Tippy and Mitch or even at my feet (not that he'd want to). The point is we can all sit together and still be comfortable. It's great, and I love it!

What I didn't love was the preparation that had to be made before we could bring the furniture home. The old furniture had to be dealt with. A few things had to be rearranged. And a lot of cleaning and organizing had to take place. Not my forte, but I knew it was the price I had to pay if I wanted the new furniture. So, I cleaned and organized.

During the process, I came across several things from previous business ventures that we had begun and failed to see through. Each of the businesses held great promise, or so we thought. And so we invested money and time only to find ourselves deeper in debt and more discouraged when our dreams crumbled before our eyes. As I stumbled across more and more material, my heart sickened. If only we hadn't spent all this money. . . If only these business ventures had been successful. . . Maybe if we had tried a little harder or a little longer. . . And on and on the thoughts wandered.

The next day, I was describing the process and feelings to my mother-in-law, and I made the statement, "Yeah, it was depressing stumbling across all these things we thought were the Lord's will but turned out to be major failures instead."

Her response stunned me. "I understand. We've had our share of endeavors-turned-failures, but I firmly believe the Lord was in them." She went on to explain that she believes God uses such experiences to prepare us for other things in life. For example, even though the various businesses Jason and I began flopped, I am still using many of the skills I learned through them in my writing business. Is it possible I never would have learned those skills if not for the businesses? As I listened to her explanation, I was amazed. Could God really use my failures for His glory? Furthermore, could my failures all be part of His master plan for my life?

Then I remembered the Sunday School lesson I had recently taught on Psalm 10. Verse 17 says, *Lord, thou hast heard the desire of the humble; thou wilt prepare their heart, thou wilt cause thine ear to hear.* "Thou wilt prepare their heart." How does God prepare our hearts? Through trials and tests, through successes and failures, through sorrow and joy.

I believe my mother-in-law is right. Just because we fail at something doesn't mean God wasn't in it. It could be that God is using it for our betterment. It could be His will for us to acquire the skills to use for another job or ministry. It could be His will for us to suffer failure so that we will know the sweet taste of success when it comes. I don't know. God's ways are not our ways, and I know I can't possibly comprehend the mind of God. But I'd like to believe that He uses our failures to "prepare our hearts" for something better yet to come.

WHEN LIFE GIVES YOU HARD BREAD

A few weeks ago, the Lord provided us with some free food. The food had just passed or was very near its expiration date, meaning it could no longer be sold, so it was donated to a local church (the very church at whose college I teach). Coincidence? What do you think? We were able to bring home some nice produce in the way of squash, asparagus and spinach, as well as three loaves of wholesome bread. Knowing we couldn't eat all the bread before it went bad, I did what I usually do when I buy an excess of discounted bread—I put it in the freezer.

Yesterday morning, I removed the loaf of pumpernickel from the freezer and set it on the counter to defrost so we could have it along with the pot of chili I had cooking in the crock pot. Unfortunately, many hours later, the bread felt just as hard as it did when I had first removed it from the freezer. It was thawed, but it was far from soft. I've held baseball bats that had more give than this loaf of bread. I have no idea what happened. I don't know if the bread was already stale when I froze it, or if pumpernickel is not an ideal bread for freezing. I just don't know. All I know is that we had tortilla chips and crackers with our chili for fear of breaking our teeth on the pumpernickel. (FYI, the dogs love it, so we're saving it as dog treats.)

As I lamented over my brick-like bread, a couple of thoughts passed through my mind. First off, being the week of Thanksgiving, I was reminded that unthankful people become just like that loaf of bread —hard, brittle and unmoving. Gratitude ought not be an obligation but a delight. No matter who we are and what circumstances we may find ourselves in, we all have so much to be thankful for. But when we're overcome with discontentment, we lose sight of what we have and focus only on what we don't have. In the process, our gratitude disappears. And before long, we find that our hearts have become bitter, our spirits brittle and our minds unmoving. What a sad fate! I, for one, do not want to be like that loaf of pumpernickel. I want to remain thankful, tender-hearted and moved with compassion for others.

The second thought came from something Jason said. As we tried to saw through the bread to see if the inside was as tough as the outside (no, we didn't need the chainsaw), Jason commented, "It'd make great croutons." What a wonderful outlook! Where I saw a flaw, Jason saw an opportunity. Hard bread? No big deal. Make croutons. Whether life is handing us lemons or hard bread, it's up to us what we do with them. We can fuss and complain about the unfairness of life. We can pout and give up, arguing that nothing ever works out the way we want it to. Or we can figure out how to turn the trial into a triumph. (In case you're wondering, option #3 is the correct answer.)

Is life always fair? Absolutely not. Do we sometimes have to face situations that we'd rather run from? Definitely. But in the midst of it all, is God still good? Unmistakably. Is Romans 8:28 still true? No doubt. Then what's the problem?

By the way, last night we finalized plans for our Thanksgiving dinner with my in-laws. Guess who's bringing the salad! And won't those croutons add the nicest touch. . .if the dogs don't eat it all before Thursday.

Giving thanks always for all things unto God
and the Father in the name of
our Lord Jesus Christ.
Ephesians 5:20

FIND AND REPLACE

As a full-time writer with an extremely busy schedule, I make a point of utilizing every shortcut and helpful hint I can find, provided the quality of the job doesn't suffer. When it comes to writing, one of my favorite shortcuts is a little feature in my word processing software called "Find and Replace." This little gem is a life-saver to writers, like myself, who tend to overuse certain words, change the name of a character half-way through the story, or forget the spelling of a particular name—spelling it one way in some places and a different way in others (i.e. Philip versus Phillip). Don't laugh! It happens. . . unfortunately, more often than I would like to admit. Anyway, with this handy little feature of "Find and Replace," I can do just that. In the "find" box, I type in the word/name that I want to change, and in the "replace" box, I type in what I want to change it to. Then, like magic, the software finds all the occurrences of that word and changes it to the new word. Do you have any idea how much time that saves? What a blessing!

Some days, though, I find myself wishing my brain had a "Find and Replace" feature. If it did, I could easily replace my thoughts of worry, anxiety and stress with those of peace, tranquility and trust. Bitterness, anger and frustration would be replaced with happiness, satisfaction and contentment. Gone would be the thoughts that weigh me down and the words that tear others down. In their place would be uplifting anthems of praise and encouragement toward my fellow man. Think of it, to be able to change our thoughts and emotions with the click of a button. Wouldn't that be awesome?

Unfortunately, I know of no such button (but if you do, please contact me). That being said, the Bible does offer us many other avenues to find and replace our negative thoughts and attitudes. While they are not shortcuts and thus require a lot of work, they are effective and a necessary part of any Christian life. My favorite of these is Philippians 4:8. If you've followed my writing for any length of time, you know that I refer to this verse a lot. The reason behind that is actually a bit embarrassing, but I'll share it with you nonetheless (the things I do for y'all!)

I am over-analytical to a fault. If something seems too easy, my default setting is to think that it must be a trick question. I analyze and analyze and analyze. Does this mean what I really think it means? That can't be right because that was far too easy. I feel like God is saying this, but I'm not sure if it's His voice or my own desires. See the pattern? Now, you're probably wondering what that has to do with Philippians 4:8, right? Simply this. Philippians 4:8 is blunt and to the point. There is no room for analytical thinking. There is no room for discussion or explanation. It says what it means and means what it says, and there's really no mistaking its message.

Finally, brethren, whatsoever things are true, whatsoever things are honest, whatsoever things are just, whatsoever things are pure, whatsoever things are lovely, whatsoever things are of good report; if there be any virtue, and if there be any praise, think on these things.

See what I mean? It says, "Think on these things," and then it gives us a list to go by. That's like me sending my husband to the store, handing him a list of items, and saying, "Buy these things." He doesn't have to figure out what I mean. He doesn't have to determine if there's some hidden meaning behind the word "milk." He takes the list and buys those things (and usually some extra things that catch his fancy, but we won't go there right now). My point is that Philippians 4:8 acts as our "Find and Replace" feature.

While it doesn't automatically change our thoughts and attitudes for us, it does help us to locate what belongs and what doesn't. It gives us a step-by-step checklist of what should be there and what needs to be re-placed with something else. I love that!

I'll be honest—very few writing projects go by without the use of the "Find and Replace" feature at least once. It is a valuable tool, and I take advantage of its benefits. My prayer today is that each of us will be as faithful in utilizing the Word of God to find the things that don't belong in our lives, hearts or minds and replace them with the things that do. I encourage you to begin with Philippians 4:8. It will point out the majority of the problem areas.

RISE UP AND BUILD

WHAT'S INSIDE?

If you squeeze a tube of toothpaste, what will come out? Applesauce? Unlikely. Yogurt? I don't think so. Cream cheese? I certainly hope not. What will come out? Toothpaste, of course. Why? Because that's what's inside.

What about us? When life gives us a squeeze, what comes out? The fruit of the Spirit? It should, but I'm afraid many times that's not the case. When life gives us a good squeeze, the result is often anger, bitterness, frustration, and discontentment. Why? Because unfortunately, that's what's inside us.

I once took a quiz on the fruit of the Spirit. The quiz listed all ten fruits with definitions and the numbers 1-10 out beside them. I had to evaluate myself and give myself a score on how evident the fruits were in my own life. One was the lowest, and ten was the highest. Sad to say, I couldn't give myself any 10's. Worse yet, I wasn't able to honestly give myself higher than a "6" on many of them. What an eye-opening experience that quiz was for me. I thought of myself as a good person, a nice girl, a true Christian. What I discovered was that my fruit was either dried and withered, or it had never grown at all. Since that day, I've been striving to do better.

You see, it's not enough to "do" the right things. It must start on the inside. We must "think" the right things. We must "want" the right things. The Bible says that the mouth speaks out of the abundance of the heart. In other words, whatever is on the inside is eventually going to find its way out. That's why it is so important that we fill our lives with the right things. After all, life is going to squeeze us from time to time. What comes out as a result of those squeezes is up to us (and it had better not be tooth-paste).

But the fruit of the Spirit is love, joy, peace,
longsuffering, gentleness, goodness, faith,
Meekness, temperance:
against such there is no law.
Galatians 5:22-23

RISE UP AND BUILD

LESSONS IN THE LIGHT

What I tell you in darkness, that speak ye in light: and what ye hear in the ear, that preach ye upon the housetops.
Matthew 10:27

I used this verse last Friday to remind us that we need to be telling others about Christ and not hiding our lights under a bushel. Today, I'd like to share with you another thought that struck me as I came across this verse last week in my Bible reading. This idea focuses on the first half of the verse: *What I tell you in darkness, that speak ye in light.*

It occurred to me that the opposite of this should be true in our lives as well: What I tell you in the light, that speak ye in the darkness. There's an old saying that admonishes, "Never doubt in the dark what God told you in the light." Same thing, right?

There are times I am so certain of God's will and so trusting in His will for my life that I feel I could move mountains. Those are the times in the light. Everything is clear. The path is made straight. The plans are laid out. Let's do this! But inevitably, the darkness comes. What seemed so clear now looks uncertain. The path is anything but straight. As for the plans? Who knows? While following through with God's will for my life, I somehow stumbled into a pit of indecision, and in that smothering darkness, doubts invaded my mind.

It is during these times that I often cling to one of my favorite quotes: "Feelings are very real, but that's not to say that they are always true." The darkest hour is not the time to make a decision because I know that decision would likely be based on feelings, not facts. So instead, I cling to the truth of God's Word. I go back and look at what He showed me in the light because, whether I feel like it or not, God's truth is unchanging. What He showed me in the light is still good in the dark. I can trust in that. . .much more so than I can trust in my ever-wavering feelings.

Perhaps you find yourself in a series of dark days, and you can't seem to figure out what God wants you to do. Don't panic. Trust in what God showed you in the light. Return to His Word. It will always lead and guide you. And whatever you do, don't make any hasty decisions based on your current feelings. The feelings will pass, but the results of poor decisions made in haste have a tendency to linger. Wait out the darkness, and while you're waiting, meditate on what you know, not what you feel!

RISE UP AND BUILD

THE LORD SHALL SUSTAIN THEE

Cast thy burden upon the Lord, and he shall
sustain thee: he shall never suffer
the righteous to be moved.
Psalm 55:22

I came across this verse in my Bible reading this morning, and while the passage is certainly familiar, today it was different somehow. For starters, it was just the verse I needed to hear this morning as my mind has been weighed down with anxieties and cares of the world. But secondly, the word *sustain* jumped out at me, and I found myself wondering what exactly does *sustain* mean? Being the wordsmith I am, I decided to look it up, and what I found nearly blessed my socks off.

There are several definitions of the word *sustain*, but after weeding out those that were not applicable regarding this verse and those that were somewhat redundant, I was left with these three definitions:

1) to support, hold or bear up

2) to keep (a person, the mind, etc.) from giving way, as under trial or affliction

3) to provide for by furnishing means or funds

I don't know about you, but each of these definitions brings me hope and encouragement. Through them, I am reminded that when I cast my burdens upon the Lord, He will hold me up. He will not let me fall, fail or give up, no matter how difficult the trial. And as He has promised, He will meet my need. In light of these new definitions, this verse now holds so much more comfort than it did before because it reminds me that I am in God's hands, that He has a good plan for my life, and that He is my strength, song and salvation. I'm reminded of the lyrics from an old hymn, "When all around my soul gives way, He then is all my hope and stay."

Whatever you are facing today, I encourage you to cast your burdens on the Lord and trust that He will hold you up, keep you from giving way and provide for your every need. Don't allow yourself to be swayed by your feelings and emotions or by the enormity of the circumstances surrounding you. Yes, the problem may be big, but I assure you, God is bigger. And He will sustain you. Trust in that!

RISE UP AND BUILD

DEFINING FORGIVENESS

What is forgiveness? When we say, "I forgive you," what do we truly mean? I won't hold it against you? I'll erase it from my memory? I understand why you did what you did? I acknowledge that your good still outweighs your bad? What is forgiveness all about?

For the longest time, I thought forgiveness was a combination of all the things above. I was under the impression that to forgive someone meant that I didn't hold the deed against that person and that I removed the instance from my memory. The problem with my definition, however, was that I felt I was constantly failing in the area of forgiveness. Allow me to explain.

Several years ago, I was hurt very badly by someone who claimed to be my friend. This person outright lied about me, and her lie resulted in serious trouble for me with my boss. After that event, things were never the same with that person, my boss or even my job. Since that time, I have made every effort to "forgive" her for what she did. The problem is that every time I see that person or even think about her, I can't help but think of what she did to me and how much her betrayal hurt me. Since the memory and negative feelings always returned, I assumed I just hadn't forgiven the person, and obviously my failure to forgive was a bad thing.

But recently, I heard forgiveness described in a way like I'd never heard it described before. Finally, it made sense. Finally, I no longer felt incapable of offering forgiveness. To sum it up, to forgive can be defined in three words: let it go. That doesn't mean we won't remember. We will.

It doesn't mean the wrongdoing won't still hurt. It will. What it means is that every time that wrongdoing surfaces in our minds, we make a choice to let it go. Acknowledge it, and then put it away. Forgiveness means that we don't let it fester until it causes bitterness in our hearts. It means that we don't allow the wrongdoing to affect the way we show the love of Christ to others. . .including the wrongdoer. It's the simple (albeit not easy) process of letting it go. It's over. It's done with. There's nothing about the event that can be changed. What can be changed, however, is how we allow the event to dictate our future.

Have you been hurt? I think we all have. Is there someone that stirs up memories of disappointment and anger in your heart? If so, know this—forgiveness is available to all. Don't let the actions of another rob you of peace and joy. Acknowledge the fault, but then let it go. The other person may not notice a difference, but I guarantee you will. We all need forgiveness from time to time, but let's not forget that we also need to forgive.

Let all bitterness, and wrath, and anger,
and clamour, and evil speaking,
be put away from you, with all malice:
And be ye kind one to another,
tenderhearted, forgiving one another,
even as God for Christ's sake
hath forgiven you.
Ephesians 4:31-32

THE NEW NORMAL

The word *normal* is seldom used when describing me. I will readily admit, compared to other women my age, I'm a bit out of step. While others are raising their children, I'm raising up a ministry. While they attend baby showers and school events, I attend women's seminars and writing workshops. While they work hard to maintain orderly households and clean houses, I do well to keep up with the dishes and laundry. Perhaps this is why I struggle to maintain friendships with many who are my age. I don't fit in. The conversations of school work and science fairs don't really apply to me, and when someone finally asks about my work (probably out of pity for the poor girl who's sitting there not saying anything), I'm all too happy to tell them. . . and that's when the crickets begin. Yep, everyone stares at me like I'm speaking Klingon, then one well-meaning soul says, "Well, that's nice." And suddenly, the subject changes.

Does this behavior hurt my feelings? Sometimes, but not nearly as much as it used to. Over the years, the Lord has helped me to understand that I have a God-sized dream that only I can see, so when I try to explain it to others, they just don't get it. After all, what could be so great about sitting home alone in front of a computer all day and typing a jumble of words in hopes that others will want to read them? For you, it probably doesn't seem great at all, but for me, I feel to my very core that I was made to do this, and it excites me.

Noah got it. After all, while his friends were going about their daily lives of work and family time, he was building a ginormous boat miles away from the nearest water. Talk about an oddball! But Noah had a God-sized dream, and he wasn't about to let a little ridicule keep him from accomplishing it.

Abraham knew what it was like to risk everything for the sake of following God's direction. When God told him to leave his home and go to a different land, Abraham didn't question. Without even knowing where he was going, he gathered his belongings and set off on a journey to follow his dream. Did others question his behavior? I'm sure. Did some call him a weirdo (or whatever the Hebrew version of weirdo is)? More than likely. But it didn't stop him.

Joseph understood. While his brothers were out watching the sheep, Joseph was dreaming lofty dreams of ruling over the land. His brothers thought he was a dork, but Joseph didn't care. He knew the dream that weighed heavily on his heart and was willing to go through a lot of tribulation to see it fulfilled.

What about you? Are you sensing that God is calling you toward a God-sized dream? Perhaps you are, but you're fearing the unknown. What will your friends say? Will your family understand?   What if you look like a fool? Join the club! I know there are many who don't understand my calling or the sacrifices that my husband and I both make to ensure that I follow this dream, but that's okay. They don't have to understand. As long as I'm doing what God called me to do, that's all that matters, and the same goes for you. Don't worry about what others will think or say. So what if they think you're not normal?   Who cares, and who are they to judge what's normal?

You do what God has set before you, and let Him take care of the results. As for the opinion of others, well, we could start our own little club. We'll call it "The Club of the New NoRmAL," and we'll only allow misfits to join (kind of like David in the cave of Adullam, I Samuel 22:2). So there! We may be weird, but at least we'll be weird together. But more than that, we'll be satisfied knowing that we've been obedient to God's will. In the end, that's all that really matters.

For do I now persuade men, or God? or do I
seek to please men? for if I yet pleased
men, I should not be the servant of Christ.
Galatians 1:10

RISE UP AND BUILD

MEDIUM, NOT RARE

I bet when you read that title, you pictured a nice, big steak sizzling on the grill or maybe a thick, juicy hamburger. Are you hungry yet? Well, sorry to ruin your drooling, but this devotion isn't about grilling or even food, for that matter. It's about people. To be more precise, Christians. And if you really want to boil it down, it's about us.

The word "medium" denotes a middle ground. It's not small or large; it's somewhere in between. In the case of food, it's not well-done or rare; it's in between. Ah, the land of in between. Are you familiar with it? The children of Israel were.

In the story of their deliverance out of Egypt, they declared—not once or twice, but multiple times—"Oh, that we were back in Egypt." Why, oh why would they want to return to a life of slavery? Honestly, it's because they were content with the middle ground. True, things in Egypt weren't great, but they could be worse, right? In the wilderness, they didn't have a clue what was going on. At least in Egypt, they knew what to expect. So, when faced with the choice of a life of slavery or a life of uncertainty, they opted for Egypt.

I'm sorry to tell you this, but we're guilty of doing the same. We, too, can be lulled into the contentment of the middle ground. Think about it for a moment. Are there changes in your life that you know you need to make, but there's really not enough incentive for you to make them?

The job isn't the best, but it could be worse, so you stick it out.

Your health isn't where you know it could be, but it could be worse, so you continue down the road of unhealthy eating habits.

Your marriage isn't all it could be, but overall, things are working, so you don't do anything to rock the boat.

You feel the Lord calling you to take a step of faith, but the fear of falling keeps your feet firmly glued in place.

Do any of these sound familiar? They do to me. Somewhere along the way, Christians have adopted the philosophy of "If it ain't broke, don't fix it." And while that sounds good in theory, it's Biblically incorrect. John 10:10 tells us, *The thief cometh not, but for to steal, and to kill, and to destroy: I am come that they might have life, and that they might have it more abundantly.*

Life more abundantly! Not life that's not too bad but could be better. Not a ho-hum existence. Not an endure-it-but-don't-enjoy-it kind of life. Christ came that we could have life more abundantly, but it will require some work and decisions on our part, and I think that's why we're content in our discontentment—because we're not willing to put in the time, effort and faith that's required to make a change. After all, the perfect job is not likely to fall in our lap. Ideal health won't simply come to us; we have to eat right and exercise. Our marriages won't improve unless we spend time on improving them by setting aside time to be together with our spouse and communicate with one another. And that step of faith? Well, if God pushed us off that precipice of uncertainty, it wouldn't be a step of faith, would it?

Now, before you throw something at me, let me say that putting time, effort and faith into these things won't make all our problems go away. In fact, it may even open the door to new challenges. That's just life, but the point is to move forward in faith and stop being content to sit in the middle. No, we can't necessarily change the circumstances, but we can change our attitudes in the midst of those circumstances. We can decide that we're tired of being slaves to convenience and knowing what to expect and we're ready to step out in faith and follow wherever God leads.

Yes, there are far too many Christians happy with the medium, and for that reason, being medium is not rare! Be unique. Live the abundant life that God has promised you, and don't look back.

So then because thou art lukewarm,
and neither cold nor hot,
I will spue thee out of my mouth.
Revelation 3:16

RISE UP AND BUILD

SEIZE THE DAY

My first thought this morning was not "What a beautiful day!" My first comment was not "Thank you, Lord, for a good night's sleep." The first idea that struck me was not "Isn't it wonderful to be alive?" I wish I could claim to be that spiritual, but alas, I cannot. And it's not because it's Monday. I know Mondays get a bad stigma, but I have nothing against Mondays. No, it wasn't the day that had me in a foul mood, but rather what I knew the day held.

Last week, I promised myself I would get some things done and caught up this week. Today marks the beginning of the week, and my "to-do" list for today alone is a mile long. There are errands to run, articles to write and marketing to complete. The laundry basket is overflowing. There's a wedding shower to plan, dinner arrangements to be made, a meeting to attend. And my house—well, let's just say I won't be winning any "Housekeeper of the Year" awards any time soon.

As I lay in bed this morning, I thought of all that needed to be done, and my heart sank. *I just want to sleep*, I thought. *I'm so very tired. Everyone needs to rest every now and then, right? Why must every day be so hectic?* Truthfully, I wanted nothing more than to pull the covers over my head and go back to sleep. I wanted to sleep away my worries and cares. I wanted to dream rather than do.

But then I was reminded of the title of a book on my bookshelf: **Every Day Deserves a Chance**. I realized that I had used my attitude to doom the day before it had even begun. I didn't give the day a chance to be a good day. I took one look at my day's obligations and allowed my feelings of fatigue and stress to dictate the kind of day I was going to have. I had the chance to make it a good day, and I blew it! Instead of giving up on the day, I should have taken my thoughts and concerns to the Lord. I could have showed Him my "to-do" list and explained how overwhelmed I was feeling. I could have asked for strength and energy to conquer the items on my list. I could have handled it so much better, but I didn't give the day a chance.

There's nothing I can do about today. I started it off wrong, and I'm trying to make the best of it now. That's all I can do. But I have a goal for tomorrow. Tomorrow morning, when I awake, I pray the Lord will bring to my mind Psalm 118:24. *This is the day which the LORD hath made; we will rejoice and be glad in it.* I hope I will then commit my day to the Lord and allow Him to guide me through each task.

Did you give today a chance? Are you allowing your doubts or worries to dictate the kind of day you'll have? Remember that every day is a gift from the Lord.   Let's not waste any!

THE MESSAGE IN THE MUSIC

This morning as I was loading the dishwasher and placing dinner in the crockpot, I was talking to the Lord, but I kept getting distracted by a song that was floating around in my head. That song led to another and then another, and before long, I realized I had stopped praying altogether and was simply serenading myself and anyone else who cared to listen. When I realized how distracted I had become, I was—at first—upset with myself, but the more I thought about what I was singing, the more I realized that I was still praying and worshiping the Lord, just in a different way.

At that point, I had to stop and thank the Lord for music. I know that may sound silly to you, but when I think about all the times God has used a song to see me through a difficult time, I'm amazed. I appreciate soft instrumental music that gets my heart focused on God and quiets my spirit so I can hear His still, small voice. I enjoy music that lightens my heart and sets my toes to tapping because of the joy that has worked its way from my heart to my foot. I cherish the songs that remind me of God's sacrifice on the cross, of His promises to me and of the heavenly home for which I long. Yes, to me, music is an indescribable blessing, and this morning I felt I needed to take a moment to thank the Lord for it.

I admit, I felt a little silly. I mean, who thanks God for music? Well, I did, and evidently, God appreciated it because when I sat down to read my daily devotions I was met with this title: **Something Special About a Song**. The devotional went on to discuss Ephesians 5:19 which states, *Speaking to yourselves in psalms and hymns and spiritual songs, singing and* *making melody in your heart to the Lord.* Coincidence? Nah, I don't believe in those. I think it was God's way of reminding me to give thanks in everything, no matter how small, insignificant or silly it may seem. He longs for our joy and our praise, and if something makes us happy, we ought to let Him know about it, right?

The fact of the matter is that I have a song to sing. . .several, in fact. I only need to be careful that unwanted melodies don't wiggle their way into my repertoire. In other words, I don't want **His Eye Is on the Sparrow** to be replaced with **Nobody Knows the Trouble I've Seen**. Singing and making melody in our heart is a good thing, as long as it's the right kind of melody. Good melodies should encourage, enlighten and help you feel at peace. They should draw your focus to God and to His Word. Bad melodies turn your focus to yourself, your problems and worldly solutions to those problems. They stir up feelings of discouragement, bitterness and rebellion.

Whether you can sing or play an instrument or struggle to carry a tune in a bucket, we all have a song to sing. The question is, what kind of song is it? Is it making a melody in our hearts to the Lord or to something altogether different?

Thank you, Lord, for giving us music to calm our hearts and restore our souls. Thank you for the joy it brings and for the opportunity You give us to sing praises unto You. But most of all, Lord, I want to thank you for the song in the night, the one that reminds us of Your loving care and encourages us to keep on keeping on. May we never take it for granted, and may we ever be mindful of the message in the music.

I call to remembrance my song in the night:
I commune with mine own heart: and my
spirit made diligent search.
Psalm 77:6

A GOOD PLACE TO STOP

God has given me the privilege and duty to write the things that He lays on my heart, but frankly, sometimes those things are not easy to write. It's not always easy to open up my heart and pour out those feelings that I would rather keep inside. Still, I know God has a purpose for them, and He has shown me, in various ways, that He uses this ministry to encourage others. Knowing that makes it all worth it.

Sticking with the theme that's been running rampant through my latest writings, I want to share with you a little "hallelujah moment" the Lord gave me the other day. As is common, I was reading. In fact, I was nearing the end of a rather exciting fiction book about a Christian archaeologist and his two children who were solving a mystery in the deserts of Africa. Jason arrived home after a long, grueling day at work, and I wanted to be able to give him my complete attention. It was bad enough that I was only a chapter and a half from the end of the book, but it really rubs me raw to have to stop reading in the middle of the chapter.

Trying to be a good wife and put my own pet peeves aside, I read to the end of the paragraph, then placed my bookmark in the book and closed it, determined to give my husband the attention he deserved. But Jason knows me all too well.

"Go ahead and get to a good stopping place," he urged.

"I read to the end of the paragraph," I assured him. "I can stop there."

He shook his head. "That's not a good stopping place. Get to the end of the chapter. You know that's a good place to stop."

By that point, I didn't care whether I finished the book or not (well, not too much). Something Jason said struck a chord within me, and it was like I finally saw the light. Crazy enough, it was something I had known all along. The end of the chapter is a good stopping place. So, could that be why God is not allowing me to get to the end of this particular chapter in my life? Could it be that's why this valley has stretched on for so long? Could it be that this rut is actually a blessing?

Like all things in life, running the Christian race requires momentum, and once we stop, even if it's just to take a rest, we have to gain that momentum all over again, right? Maybe God is doing me a favor by keeping me going. While I'm not exactly enjoying my time in the valley, I'm learning a lot along the way, and I've certainly gained some momentum. There will be an end to this valley, and there will be a "good place to stop," but I haven't arrived yet.

As Jason's words echoed in my head and my heart, it was as if that still, small voice of the Lord said, "Yeah, Dana. Get to the end of the chapter. You can't stop in the middle. You'll know when it's the right time to stop."

The crazy part for me is that once I stop reading a book, even though I found a good stopping place, I can't wait to pick it up and start reading it again. Perhaps the Christian walk can be the same way. By going when we're supposed to go and stopping when we're supposed to stop, we not only gain momentum, but we also gain a desire to continue the journey. And with that mindset, the end of the race will be here before we know it.

There is a good place to stop, but you may not be there yet. Hang in there. God will lead you through to the end of the chapter. Until then, enjoy the story. After all, it's not just about the destination; it's also about the journey.

Now, if you'll excuse me, I have another book to read, and I'm pretty sure that once I start, I won't want to put it down.

I have taught thee in the way of wisdom; I have led thee in right paths. When thou goest, thy steps shall not be straitened; and when thou runnest, thou shalt not stumble.
Proverbs 4:11-12

RISE UP AND BUILD

ON THE OTHER SIDE OF A MIRACLE

Have you ever felt that your life was like a puzzle with one or more missing pieces? Like if you could fill those voids, your life would be complete? Perhaps you've thought, *If only I had that job, then I'd be happy.* Or maybe, *If only I were married, then my life would be perfect.* Or how about, *If only I had more money, then I could be satisfied*? We don't want much, just a miracle here or there. And we've convinced ourselves that if God would just see fit to give us our miracle, we'd be completely happy and never need to ask for anything ever again. But according to the Bible, it doesn't work that way. Take a look:

And Ahab told Jezebel all that Elijah had done, and withal how he had slain all the prophets with the sword. Then Jezebel sent a messenger unto Elijah, saying, So let the gods do to me, and more also, if I make not thy life as the life of one of them by to morrow about this time. And when he saw that, he arose, and went for his life, and came to Beersheba, which belongeth to Judah, and left his servant there. But he himself went a day's journey into the wilderness, and came and sat down under a juniper tree: and he requested for himself that he might die; and said, It is enough; now, O Lord, take away my life; for I am not better than my fathers. - I Kings 19:1-4

It is obvious that Elijah was in a severe state of depression. He was so distraught that he wanted to die. He had had enough. He was tired of running for his life. He was tired of being alone (although he was never really alone). He was ready to quit. But the thing that's so astounding is the timing of his depression. It was not at a time when he was in desperate straits. Sure,

Jezebel wanted to kill him, but that was nothing new. Ahab had been trying to get a hold of Elijah for the past three years, but God prevented Elijah from being found. Surely, God could/would have continued his protection of the prophet. But these feelings of desperation and despair took place right on the heels of Elijah's "big miracle"—you know, the one where he called down fire from Heaven which burnt up the altar and everything on, under and around it. The one that turned Israel back to God.

Elijah had just seen (and not for the first time) the power of God. He had witnessed His protection over and over again. He knew God's faithfulness and goodness. He had been a recipient of God's provision on more than one occasion. Elijah had every reason to be on Cloud Nine. He had gotten, not one, but many miracles. He asked, and God gave. He should have been thrilled, but he wasn't.

Perhaps Elijah had the same mindset we do, that the missing miracle would be the piece that would complete the puzzle that was his life. But when the miracle was over and he still felt incomplete, perhaps he realized that not only was he still missing *a piece* but he was also missing *peace*. The miracle didn't fill the void. The very thing he thought would make him happy didn't. And so, Elijah found himself not only discouraged but also disappointed.

My friend, it is so easy in this life to want the things that we do not have, but we must be careful that we don't seek after those things in order to fill a void that only God can fill. If He wants us to have "that miracle," then we will, but we must not allow our happiness and life's purpose to depend on it. In other words, we shouldn't put as much weight on what God does for us as we do on who He is to us. Miracles have their place, and while they will bring temporary joy, more of life's problems will quickly drain that joy away. However, if we will keep our eyes on who God is—the one everlasting joy —then we will be content and happy with or without "that miracle."

There's nothing wrong with praying for a miracle, nor is there anything wrong with waiting for it. The problem occurs when we place the miracle above the Miracle Worker. Only God can fill those missing pieces of our lives and, in so doing, supply the missing peace in our hearts. Seek Him today, not simply what He can do for you. Then everything else will fall into place.

But seek ye first the kingdom of God, and his righteousness; and all these things shall be added unto you.
Matthew 6:33

RISE UP AND BUILD

PUT THAT KNOWLEDGE TO WORK

During our devotion time last night, Jason and I were reading from Oswald Chamber's book, **My Utmost for His Highest**. Unlike many of his short devotions, this particular one was so straightforward and to the point that it really left no room for discussion. The focus of the message was clear: it's not enough to know to do good; we must put that knowledge in action. The only thing I could think to say at the conclusion of the reading was that I was surprised he didn't use Philippians 4:9 as one of his key verses: *Those things, which ye have both learned, and received, and heard, and seen in me, do: and the God of peace shall be with you.*

Jason agreed, and we carried on with our devotions and prayer time.

This morning, as I did my personal devotions, guess what verse I came across. Yep, you guessed it—Philippians 4:9. I laughed and sent Jason a text with the verse and the sentence, "Sound familiar?" He sent back a smiley face. God was doing it again. He was using multiple sources to drive home a singular point. But as I pondered the verse this morning, I felt a bit like Princess Mia in *The Princess Diaries* where she says, "The concept is grasped; the execution is a little elusive."

I understand the verse. I know what it says and what it means. It makes perfect sense to me. However, carrying out that particular order sometimes seems very difficult, and for the life of me, I can't figure out why. I guess it's the flesh. I want to serve God. I want to do the things He's taught me to do and avoid the things He's told me to avoid. Yet when faced with certain circumstances, I make the wrong choice. I choose the chocolate cake over the fruit or the soda over water. I choose the easy way instead of the right way. I choose my feelings over what I know to be true. I choose anger instead of forgiveness, bitterness over goodness and selfishness over selflessness. I know better. I really do. But still I make the wrong choice. Fortunately, God's still working on me and helping me to do those things I need to do.

I remind you today that it's not enough to <u>know</u> what's right; we must also <u>do</u> what's right. Knowledge is great, but unless we put it into practice, it's pretty much worthless. I know it isn't easy, but with God all things are possible. We can do this in His strength. We need only be willing.

But be ye doers of the word, and not hearers only, deceiving your own selves. For if any be a hearer of the word, and not a doer, he is like unto a man beholding his natural face in a glass: For he beholdeth himself, and goeth his way, and straightway forgetteth what manner of man he was. But whoso looketh into the perfect law of liberty, and continueth therein, he being not a forgetful hearer, but a doer of the work, this man shall be blessed in his deed.
James 1:22-25

WHAT A TANGLED WEB!

I walked through a spiderweb this morning. That, in and of itself, is not unusual. What is odd is that I wasn't outside at the time. No, this spiderweb was in my house. And it was not a little web by any means. No, this web had its own zip code. It stretched from my curtains to my mantel and then down to my stereo.

Now, I will be the first to admit that I haven't won any "Housekeeper of the Year" awards. In fact, my housekeeping leaves A LOT to be desired (sorry, Mom). Nevertheless, I do frequently take the time to rid my house of spiderwebs. The problem is that we live in a very old house which means there are a lot of cracks and crevices for pesky little critters to enter in. And enter in they do. I can be completely rid of spider-webs in the morning, but by afternoon, my house resembles the ancient crypts. It's un-real how quickly and elaborately these spiders can spin their webs.

You know who else is good at spin-ning webs? Satan. He can spin webs of dis-couragement, discontentment, and doubt better than any spider alive. The tricky part about these webs is that, like the web I walked through this morning, they often show up in unexpected places. Before we realize what's happening, we're tangled in a sticky web for which we were unprepared.

For this reason, the Bible tells us to always be on guard. "Watch and pray," Je-sus said. "Put on the whole armor of God." Over and over again, we are warned to ex-pect the unexpected. When we do, we are less likely to become snared in one of Sa-tan's webs.

As you get ready for the day today, be sure to grab your armor, your sword, and your shield. You may be facing fiery darts, but also be on guard for the unseen webs that may be in your path. They can often be as dangerous (and sometimes more) than the fiery darts. Beware!

Wherefore take unto you the whole armour of God, that ye may be able to withstand in the evil day, and having done all, to stand.
Ephesians 6:13

RISE UP AND BUILD

IS YOUR COMMUNION ALL ABOUT THE WHINE?

When I did a quick search on the word "communion," I came up with two separate definitions:

1) the service of Christian worship at which bread and wine are consecrated and shared.
2) the sharing or exchanging of intimate thoughts and feelings, especially when the exchange is on a mental or spiritual level.

The first is a rite of the church, also known as the Lord's Supper. It is the time set aside to remember Christ's great sacrifice on the cross and to follow the Lord's command, "This do ye in remembrance of me." In keeping with the tradition, the congregation takes part in the eating of the bread and the drinking of the wine (grape juice). And while this is an important and sacred event, it is not the form of communion I wish to discuss this morning, though I do want to make a play on words when asking, "Is your communion all about the whine?"

The communion I wish to discuss today is that of exchanging intimate thoughts and feelings, particularly with the Lord in prayer. Each day, we are privileged with an open invitation to approach God's throne and invited to stay as long as we want. During that time, we are urged to pour out our hearts before the Lord, to share our innermost thoughts and desires, to express our deepest joys. But I wonder if I'm the only one who has a tendency to make that communion all about the whine.

I don't mean to. I don't approach the throne of God ready to dump all my prob-

lems on Him, but within just a couple of minutes in prayer, the whine takes over. Instead
of asking for the Lord to meet my needs, I
whine about what I don't have. Instead of
interceding on my brother or sister's behalf, I
whine about how my problems are bigger
than theirs. Instead of lifting up my voice in
praise, I whine about how long it's taking the
Lord to answer my prayers. Whine, whine,
whine! And then I wonder why I leave my
prayer closet feeling discouraged and overwhelmed. What should I expect?

Recently, I was introduced to a new
way to pray. While I don't necessarily use
this format every day, I have found that it
helps keep my thoughts more focused, my
prayers less self-centered, and my whines to
a minimum. And my favorite thing is that it's
easy to remember. Just think "P.R.A.I.S.E."

The "P" stands for praise. Before I
ask for anything or whine about my lot in life,
I praise the Lord for who He is and what
He's done in my life. Believe it or not, by the

time I spend just a few minutes here, I find I have much less to complain about than before I began.

The "R" stands for repent. Doing this regularly, I keep short accounts with God, which is imperative for our relationship. And oddly enough, I find that it's the same couple of things each time, which helps me pinpoint the spiritual areas in my life that need the most work. Repentance puts me in a more humble state and helps me to realize that I don't deserve anything from God, so everything He gives is a blessing far beyond what I could ever deserve. It changes my entire attitude.

The "A" is for acknowledgment. Again, this is all about attitude and frame of mind. During this time, I acknowledge that God is the Lord of all and that He is in control of all things. No matter what I may face, I can rest assured that it has passed through His hands first. I acknowledge that He is the Master, and I am the servant, subject to His commands. Do you see how this type of prayer is pulling our eyes off ourselves and on the Lord?

The "I" stands for intercession. This is the time spent praying for others. Obviously, I can't pray for everybody every day, so instead, I either divide up my prayer list, or I pray for the specific needs the Lord lays on my heart.

The "S" is for supplication. Now, it's time for me to pour out my personal requests. Yes, sometimes, I do still whine, especially if I have a need that is weighing me down, but for the most part, I find that I simply state my needs and requests to God. Most of the "whine" has dissipated by the time I reach this point of my prayer.

Lastly, the "E" stands for equipping. Before leaving the throne of God, I ask for the Lord to equip me with the specific things I need to live for Him that day. Maybe it's strength or focus or a calm spirit. Whatever the need, I ask Him to equip me to face the day ahead.

Is this the perfect prayer formula? Probably not. Does it eliminate the whine altogether? I'm afraid not. But, as I mentioned before, it does keep my thoughts focused and my prayer life less self-centered. By doing that, I've found that the whines are contained to a minimum.

What about you? Is your communion all about the whine? Maybe you ought to try a different approach to your time with the Lord. Who knows? Perhaps you'll find a way to eliminate the whines completely. (If you do, would you please let me know? That's something I'm definitely interested in.)

The Lord is nigh unto all them that call upon him, to all that call upon him in truth.
Psalm 145:18

LOOK TO THE SKIES

Have you ever doubted God's faithfulness? I know it's not an easy thing to admit. God is so good to us and so holy that we feel guilty admitting that we have, on occasion, doubted that He would do what He said He would do. Typically, these doubts come during some of life's harshest storms when it seems the sun will never shine again. But what we often fail to realize during these times is that just because the clouds fill the skies doesn't negate the fact that the sun is still there. Hidden from view, yes, but there nonetheless, and no amount of cloud cover can change that.

I will sing of the mercies of the Lord for ever: with my mouth will I make known thy faithfulness to all generations. For I have said, Mercy shall be built up for ever: thy faithfulness shalt thou establish in the very heavens. - Psalm 89:1-2

I can't tell you how many times I've read through the Psalms, but it wasn't until last week that the last phrase of verse two caught my attention. I truly believe God reveals these heavenly nuggets to us at the times we need them the most. Last week was a tough week for me, and while there was a lot coming out of my mouth, it certainly wasn't praise or worship. No, it was more like complaints and pleading to discover why God had turned His back on me. And in the midst of my doubt-laden storm, I found this truth: *thy faithfulness shalt thou establish in the very heavens*.

Many times in this life what we feel will collide with what we know. And in those confusing times, we often find our moods and actions dictated by our feelings and emotions. We feel like God has forsaken us, so we act accordingly. But according to this wonderful verse in the Psalms, God has given us unmistakable proof that He is and always will be faithful. In fact, every time the sun rises and sets, we can be reminded of God's faithfulness. Just as our feelings can't deter the setting or rising of the sun, neither can they change the faithfulness of God. It is always there, perhaps hidden by my clouds of doubt, but there nonetheless. And to make sure we never lose sight of that, He gives us daily reminders. The rise and fall of the sun. The phases of the moon. The twinkle of the stars. Not only do the heavens declare the glory of God, but they also declare His faithfulness. Day after day, night after night, God gives us unequivocal proof that He can be relied upon.

Are you feeling forsaken today? Do you find yourself wondering if God is still faithful? If so, look to the skies. Did the sun set last night? Did it rise this morning? Did the moon follow its proper course around the earth? Yes, yes and yes. So, is God still faithful? I think you know the answer.

It is of the Lord's mercies that we are not consumed, because his compassions fail not. They are new every morning: great is thy faithfulness.
Lamentations 3:22-23

SAME VERSE—NEW MEANING

Create in me a clean heart, O God;
and renew a right spirit within me.
Psalm 51:10

For most of my adult life, this has been one of my favorite verses. In fact, I often use it as a prayer. Unfortunately, I often find it necessary to pray for a clean heart and a right attitude. And until recently, that's all I really saw in this verse.

Create in me a clean heart - "Lord, forgive me of my sins and wash my heart clean. It's simple. It's basic. It's to the point. I've done wrong. My heart is dirty. Please clean it."

Renew a right spirit within me - "Lord, help my attitude. I'm having a lot of trouble with it right now. I'm angry and bitter. I'm jealous or covetous. My attitude is not right, and I want to get it right before I say something I'll regret. This attitude is not helpful, nor is it pleasing to You. Please renew a right attitude in my heart."

If that were all I ever gleaned from this verse, it would be enough. But through a recent trial, God showed me another nugget to which I could cling. You see, throughout this entire ordeal, I've been struggling. Not with anger or bitterness. Not with discontentment. Not with discouragement. No, I've been struggling with fear. The "what if's" have been knocking at my door constantly. What if this? What if that? Day and night, my mind has been filled with nagging questions and suffocating doubts.

When I say that I've been struggling with fear, let me elaborate. I haven't just been afraid. I've been downright terrified at times. I'm talking scared to the point of shaking so bad I could barely stand and being so sick to my stomach that I was sure I was going to lose my lunch. The gnawing sensation within me was paralyzing and sickening.

During one of my attacks, God brought to mind another powerful verse: *For God hath not given us the spirit of fear; but of power, and of love, and of a sound mind. (II Timothy 1:7)* At that moment, the two verses seemed to collide, and I saw something I'd never seen before. When I pray, "Renew a right spirit within me," it goes far beyond just fixing my attitude. It goes much deeper than that. It means fixing my entire spirit. Now, when I pray that prayer, instead of just thinking of an improved attitude, I realize that I am asking God to take away my fear and to replace it with power, love and a sound mind.

You see, God is not the author of fear. It doesn't come from Him. It is not of Him. By allowing it to rule my thoughts and actions, I was allowing it to take the place of God in my life. I was allowing it to become my master. For me, this is unacceptable.

Am I still fearful? From time to time, yes. Is that fear still gripping? Most definitely. So, what's changed? The way I handle it. I now know how to pray. I know what to pray for. I know what kind of spirit I need. And above all, I know the One who can give me that spirit. It's up to me, however, to ask.

WHAT YOU SEE ISN'T NECESSARILY WHAT YOU GET

A few weeks ago, I came across a quote by Henry David Thoreau that states, "It's not what you look at that matters; it's what you see." That statement has stuck with me over the past weeks, and yesterday, the Lord even brought it to life right before my eyes.

I was returning from my prayer walk when I noticed a bird sitting in the shadows in the middle of the road ahead of me—at least, I thought it was a bird. I could clearly see its head, beak, body and extended tail. Oddly enough, it was just sitting there. It didn't fly away. It didn't bend over to scoop up some tasty bug off the ground. It didn't even hop around to see what was available. It just sat there perfectly still until a gust of wind knocked it over, beak-first, onto the ground. Only then did I realize that the "bird" was actually a leaf. Perhaps it's time for an eye appointment, huh?

That being said, I'm sure you've done the same thing—saw something that you thought was one thing only to find out it was another. Come on, admit it. Don't make me feel alone in this thing. I already feel crazy enough for seeing a bird where there wasn't one. Maybe it's stress or lack of sleep. All I know is that as soon as I realized my mistake, God brought Thoreau's quote back to my mind. I was looking at a leaf, but I saw a bird.

How many times in life do we make the same mistake in spiritual matters? We look at a problem, but we see a mountain. We look at a diagnosis, but we see a death sentence. We look at the pink slip, but we see financial ruin. Unfortunately, we even do it with God. We look at Him, and we see a God who <u>used to do</u> great things. It's not what we look at that's causing our spiritual struggles in life; it's what we see. We see what we think is inevitable. We see the worst outcome. We see what we fear. But are we seeing the truth, or are we—like I did yesterday—seeing something that isn't there?

I propose we start living life by another statement: "It's not what you see that matters; it's what God sees." The God who parted the Red Sea, healed the sick, raised the dead and cast out demons. The God who is above all and more powerful than we could possibly imagine. What does He see? I would suggest that when He looks at your problem, He sees the walls of Jericho, ready to tumble. When He sees the diagnosis, He sees the chance to prove His grace whether in healing here on earth or in Heaven. When He sees the pink slip, He sees the opportunity to move you to another place where you can better serve Him and probably be much happier in the process. Where we see boulders, God sees pebbles. Where we see oceans, He sees a water fountain. I dare say if we saw what He did, we wouldn't be afraid.

The trouble is we can't see what He sees. We don't have the same vantage point. But I'll tell you what we can do—we can trust. If He says He's got it under control, let's take Him at His word. If He says He'll supply our every need, then let's agree that He means it. We may be blinded to the reality of our situation, but God is not. He is fully aware of what is taking place, not only now, but down the road as well. He can see around the bend, so let's stop living our lives based on what we see and instead trust in what God sees. That should keep us from making mountains out of molehills. . . or birds out of leaves!

*What shall we then say to these things? If
God be for us, who can be against us?
Romans 8:31*

RISE UP AND BUILD

ARE YOU WALKING IN CIRCLES?

Do you ever feel like you're walking in circles? You're trying to live right, serve God and follow his will, but for the life of you, you can't seem to keep on track. Or maybe you think you are on track, only to find you've veered way off course. I saw an excellent example of this the other day on **Myth-Busters**.

I don't know if you've ever watched the show, but the premise is that this group of scientists perform various tests to prove or disprove a myriad of myths. On this particular episode, the myth was that it is impossible to travel in a straight line while blindfolded, so the scientists put it to the test. At first, they blindfolded themselves and tried walking in a straight line toward a predetermined point. The results were astounding. Not only could they not travel in a straight line, but they spent most of their time actually walking in circles.

Next, they tried swimming. With blindfolds in place, they set out across a narrow channel to see if they could reach the other side. Once again, before they had traveled far, each of them was veering off course, and eventually, they began traveling in circles once again.

Lastly, they tried driving while blindfolded. (Please do not try this at home. They are professionals and were performing this test in a safe location where they could not hurt anyone or themselves.) Each of the scientists had their doubts that they would veer off course when driving a car. After all, all you have to do is hold the steering wheel still, and the vehicle should track true. But that was not the case. While their travels weren't as haphazard as their other attempts, their course was anything but a straight line. Thus, the myth was confirmed. It is impossible to travel in a straight line while blindfolded.

When we walk by faith and not by sight, we are essentially blindfolded, and without the guidance of the Holy Spirit, it is impossible to travel straight and true. This is why Proverbs 3:5-6 is in the Bible: *Trust in the Lord with all thine heart; and lean not unto thine own understanding. In all thy ways acknowledge him, and he shall direct thy paths.*

The Lord warns us not to lean on our understanding but to trust Him to direct our paths. When the scientists were performing this test, they declared several times that they could feel themselves being pulled in a particular direction, but when they said they felt pulled to the left, they were actually veering to the right. But based on their understanding of what was happening, they instinctively corrected their course by pulling to the right because they felt they were veering to the left. This resulted in them getting further and further off course and eventually traveling in circles.

If we're not careful, we can do the same. Focused on our own understanding of the situation, we can make hasty judgments and end up getting further off course in our spiritual race. It may seem like we need to go left when, in actuality, we need to go right. It may feel like we need to wait, but God says it's time to move. It may seem like the time to speak, but it's actually the time to be quiet and listen. Our own understanding is fickle and is easily influenced by so many factors surrounding us, including our feelings. Our own thoughts cannot be trusted. That's what faith is all about. It's not about believing in what we see, hear or feel, but rather believing in God. Faith allows God to direct our paths, And faith is what we need to finish our race. Otherwise, we may find ourselves endlessly traveling in circles, always going but never getting anywhere. And

that, my friend, makes for a very weary
Christian!

RISE UP AND BUILD RESOURCES

If you enjoyed this book and would like to find out more about dealing with anxiety and depression, I encourage you to pick up the other books in the series: *Rise Up and Build* and *Rise Up and Build Good Health*. Each of these books builds on the principles established in this book, giving you resources to heal your body, mind and spirit.

If you're looking for additional ways to combat anxiety and depression, I invite you to visit RiseUpandBuild.net, where you'll find numerous free resources to aid you in your battle toward freedom.

ABOUT THE AUTHOR

Dana Rongione is the author of several Christian books, including the highly-praised **Giggles and Grace** devotional series for women. A dedicated wife and doggie "mom," Dana lives in Greenville, SC, where she spends her days writing and reaching out to the hurting and discouraged. Connect with her on her website, DanaRongione.com, and be sure to sign up for her daily devotions.

BOOKS BY DANA RONGIONE

Devotional/Christian Living:

He's Still Working Miracles: Daring To Ask God for the Impossible

There's a Verse for That

'Paws'itively Divine: Devotions for Dog Lovers

The Deadly Darts of the Devil

What Happened To Prince Charming?: Ten Tips to Achieve a Happy Marriage Life and Live Happily Ever After

Rise Up and Build Devotional: 52 Inspirational Thoughts for Dealing with Anxiety and Depression

Giggles and Grace Series:

Random Ramblings of a Raving Redhead

Daily Discussions of a Doubting Disciple

Lilting Laments of a Looney Lass

Mindful Musings of a Moody Motivator

Other Titles for Adults:

Rise Up and Build: A Biblical Approach To Dealing With Anxiety and Depression

Rise Up and Build Good Health: Practical Insights to Heal Your Emotions by Healing Your Body

Creating a World of Your Own: Your Guide to Writing Fiction

The Delaware Detectives Middle-Grade Mystery Series:

Book #1 – The Delaware Detectives: A Middle-Grade Mystery

Book #2 – Through Many Dangers

Book #3 – My Fears Relieved

Book #4 – I Once Was Lost

Books for Young Children:

Through the Eyes of a Child

God Can Use My Differences

Audio Bible Studies:

Moodswing Mania – a Bible study through select Psalms (6 CD's)

The Names of God – a 6-CD Bible study exploring some of the most powerful names of God

Miracles of the Old Testament, Part 1 – a Bible study with a unique look at miracles in the Old Testament (4 CD's)

There's a Verse for That – Scripture with a soft music background, perfect for meditation or memorization

ACKNOWLEDGMENTS

This book would not have been possible without the help and support of the following people:

The Lord, my Strength and Song — Without Him, I can do nothing!

My husband, Jason

My loyal and high-ranking patrons:
    Lewis and Sharon White
    Patty Hicks
    Dawn Hodge
    Jo Anne Hall
    Peter Santaniello
    Lisa Gutschow
    Tara Looper
    And others who wish to remain anonymous. . .

My church family who constantly asked, "When will the new book be ready?" They urged me to complete the task, no matter how overwhelming it seemed at times.

RISE UP AND BUILD

RISE UP AND BUILD

38973777R00157

Made in the USA
Columbia, SC
17 December 2018